Warm Ups for Soccer

A Dynamic Approach

by *Mick Critchell*

**Library of Congress
Cataloging - in - Publication Data**

by Mick Critchell
    Warm Ups for Soccer
        A Dynamic Approach

ISBN No. 1-59164-028-8
Lib. of Congress Catalog No. 2002110228
© 2002

Editing
Bryan R. Beaver

Printed by
DATA REPRODUCTIONS
Auburn, Michigan

Reedswain Publishing
612 Pughtown Road
Spring City, PA 19475
800.331.5191
www.reedswain.com
info@reedswain.com

Kit Symons and Joe Griffin with the author

Acknowledgements

I would to thank my friends, who gave up their time to make a massive contribution to this book.

Photographer   Alan Duffy

Graphics   Peter Qualmann

Models   Joe Griffin, Loughborough University
                          Kit Symons, Crystal Palace and Wales

SAQ   Alan Pearson and SAQ for pointing me
                          in the right direction.

Contents

Legend for Diagrams

1) ⟶   Movement of player

2) - - - - - - - ►   Movement of ball

3) ——— - - - ►   Movement of player and ball

4) ⟶   Dribbling movement of player

5) ▲   Cone   6) ⊕   Ball

7) ◄——— 10M ———►   Distance

8) ⊏⊓⊓⊓⊓⊓⊓⊐   Ladder

9) ◯ ◯ ◯ ◯   Hoops

10) ⌈ ⌈   Flagpoles

11) ⌉⌉⌉   Hurdles

Introduction

I was recently taking a training session for my local soccer club and arrived early. As I had nothing to do, I watched an under 10 soccer practice, which was taking place before mine. I was horrified by what I saw. The first 35 minutes were spent running around the outside of the astro-turf and performing shuttle runs. The coaches then talked to the players for 5 minutes before picking two teams. The last 20 minutes of the session were spent on a small-sided game across half a pitch, with both coaches joining in. No coaching was done within the game. During the whole practice, the maximum number of touches for any boy would have been about 35. With an hour in which to work, each boy should have had a minimum of 1000 touches.

Unfortunately this was not an isolated incident, but one to which I have become all too accustomed. As one international field hockey player once remarked with regard to training, "I never remember running 14 laps of the pitch when I was playing". The same principle applies to soccer, particularly when children are involved. It is the coach's job to ensure that the time available is spent wisely and this means as many touches of the ball as possible.

It is, however, the area of the warm-ups that most concerns me. All too often, the quality of the warm up is poor, with players either running to the fence and back, doing a couple of laps of the track or a lap of the pitch and then statically stretching for what seems an eternity.

For me, this was time wasted. In recent years, the use of static stretching during the pre-performance warm up has been strongly refuted by exercise physiologists who have proven the importance of flexibility and dynamic flexibility not only in soccer but in most sports.

So how could the start of training sessions be better structured? Instead of lapping the track or pitch, the training and/or pre-game warm up should start with dynamic flexibility work. This could be described as functional/movement specific flexibility for soccer. There are, however, guiding principles, which have to be adhered to when using this type of flexibility. The players must work within the current range of movement and the speed of movement should gradually increase over time. The exercises should be of good quality and based on sound posture and correct mechanics. To gain most from this type of exercise, the coach must be able to analyze the actual movements used in soccer and then include these in the warm-up.

Working in conjunction with dynamic flexibility is the skill development for soccer, which begins with the development of movement skills. The fundamental movement phase is nurtured between 2 and 10 years, mature fundamental skills overlap the latter end of this phase, whilst the soccer specific skills phase occurs from 8 upwards.

THE KEY TO MOVEMENT PATTERN IN SOCCER IS THE DEVELOPMENT OF THE SKILLS LEARNED DURING THE FUNDAMENTAL MOVEMENT PHASE.

Research has shown that children are leaving elementary school without adequate development of fundamental skills. There is clear evidence that mechanical co-ordination is neglected in the youth of this generation and this results in limited capacity to perform skills efficiently. In practice, it is possible for a player to develop soccer specific skills without having a range of fundamental skills. However in the dynamics of a game, when such a player goes beyond their narrow range of skill, problems occur. A good example of this was the England team in Euro 2000, who found it difficult to keep possession of the ball when put under intense pressure by the opposition.

It is known that older children may catch up when these fundamentals are eventually taught, even though experts agree that the sensitive period in early childhood is the easiest learning period. The onus therefore falls on the teacher or coach, not only to teach the skills involved in soccer, but also to ensure that the players practice fundamental movement skills as well. I believe the time to do this is during the warm up. Players should be taught how to run correctly and this would include acceleration, deceleration and lateral movement. Other fundamental movement patterns such as balance, eye-hand and eye-feet co-ordination as well as an awareness of time, space and own body parts and positions should also be included. We must ensure that multi-directional footwork, which underpins all games, is taught correctly and a dynamic flexibility warm up can be used for this purpose. So instead of lapping the track and statically stretching, use the time at the start of the practice to educate the players to become good movers.

Value of the Warm Up

On several occasions I have watched the opposing substitutes warming up at half time, in preparation for the second half. What amazed me was that most, if not all, of their time was spent statically stretching. I wanted to go across and say to them that warming up and statically stretching are not the same thing and what they were doing was likely to be detrimental to their second half performance. However, I didn't want to fall foul of the opposing coach or trainer, so I kept my thoughts to myself.

It needs to be made clear that static stretching and warming up are NOT the same thing. Warming up for soccer must include activities that raise the total body temperature, as well as the temperature of the muscles, in order to prepare the body for the game or training session to come. To be effective, the warm up must increase the body temperature by one or two degrees Celsius. The temperature of the blood then increases as it travels through the working muscles and this, in turn, makes more oxygen available to the working muscles since the warmer the blood, the less oxygen it can hold. The higher temperature also speeds up the process of energy production (one degree speeds up the process by 13%) and increases the elasticity of connecting muscles, joints and tendons, once viscosity is decreased. This leads to an increase in the Range of Movement (ROM).

The muscles will reach working temperatures after 10 - 15 minutes, if players are in warm surroundings or wearing tracksuits. The feeling of being totally warm does not occur until after 30 - 40 minutes and this is when the whole body has reached work temperature. The warm up should therefore last a minimum of 15 minutes and coaches can help players get warm more quickly by insisting that they wear tracksuits, particularly in cold weather. It never ceases to astound me that professional players still prepare for games, in very cold weather, wearing only shorts and T-shirts. We have to get rid of the `macho` image.

The Argument Against Static Stretching Prior to Training or Competition

Since the 1970's static stretching has become the main method of maintaining or increasing flexibility amongst soccer players, with dynamic flexibility falling out of favor. Fortunately, sports scientists from around the world have started to look at the relevant literature and carry out their own experiments and this has led them to question many of the beliefs and practices which have been promoted for so long.

In 1997, Gleim and Mchugh challenged the premise that an increase in flexibility reduced the risk of injury. A recently published article from Australia supported this view. An experiment with a large number of army recruits was carried out, with half the volunteers warming up without using static stretching, whilst the other half warmed up and statically stretched. At the end of the basic course it was found that the group who didn't use static stretching had fewer injuries than the group who did. This finding was supported by a similar experiment in Canada, which concluded that warming up prevented injury whilst static stretching had no effect on injury prevention whatsoever!

New muscle research findings from Australia support the theory that static stretching decreases muscle eccentric strength for up to an hour after the stretch (Bennett 1999). Obviously, eccentric strength is vital in the production of power for a soccer player and yet it has been shown that static stretching reduced muscular strength by 9% as long as 60 minutes after the stretch. Specific stretching of the hamstring group was shown to reduce eccentric strength by 7% (Bennett 1999).

Rosenbaum and Hennig (1995) state that static stretching reduced peak force by 5% and the rate of force production by 8%, in their study of Achilles tendon reflex activity. This is significant since Achilles tendon reflex activity is a vital mechanism in the production of explosive power for soccer players. Stainsky, Fales and Lilieenthal (1956) found that when a muscle is statically stretched, the rate of oxygen consumption fell to half its resting rate. When the stretch was released, oxygen consumption returned to previous levels, but with little repayment of the debt that was created during the stretch. Perhaps most significant of all were the findings of Gerard van der Poel, who stated that static stretching caused a deterioration in the specific co-ordination of explosive movements. Considering there are a large number of explosive movements during a game of soccer, it seems advisable not to carry out static stretching prior to a training session or game. It is also a myth that soccer players need relaxed muscles before playing. Instead they need warm, fast muscles, which are ready to cope with the physical demands of the game.

This criterion is supported by the Russian, Pavel Tsatsouline, in his book Beyond Stretching (1997). He is very critical of western physiologists and says that we would be better off not stretching than following their advice. He believes that to be flexible in motion you have to stretch in motion, eventually at the speed of your sport. Tsatsouline therefore recommends dynamic/plyometric flexibility stretching before competition, as it increases the neural input to the muscles and is the natural way for the body to operate.

Warming up is the foundation of a successful training session or game. Unfortunately, many soccer players, like all other athletes, often doubt the value of warming up and are keen to get on with the game or practice. For many, time is already too short for training, so fringe activities such as warm ups are often regarded as luxuries, which can be done without. Coaches therefore have a key role to play because they must ensure the warm up is carried out correctly, so that players are physically prepared, in order to achieve optimal performance. If the warm up is inadequate, this often leads to a poor workout or indifferent start to a game.

The Ideal Format for the Warm up

A good warm up session should be divided into three parts - dynamic flexibility, running technique and specific soccer action.

STAGE ONE   - Dynamic flexibility

For the first five minutes, the players should engage in aerobic activity so that the large muscles have to work. Jogging, running, jumping, skipping and so on appear to be the best way of doing this. The aim is simply to raise the core body temperature and get the blood flowing. At this stage the players should avoid acceleration, deceleration and sudden changes of direction.

Players then start the dynamic flexibility exercises, which, according to Thomas Kurz, "involves moving parts of the body and gradually increasing reach, speed of movement or both". It is a form of flexibility that has been used for some time in other sports, particularly track and field, but is only slowly catching on in soccer. However, it makes sense to use this method of stretching since most movement in soccer is dynamic. There are few sports in which an ability to achieve a high level of static flexibility is desirable, though activities such as gymnastics and diving might be exceptions. Interestingly though, at the recent World Gymnastic Championships, in which 86 countries took part, not one static stretch was performed prior to competition. Instead, every country had its own dynamic flexibility routine, which was carried out religiously by the gymnasts.

Dynamic flexibility consists of function-based exercises that use soc-cer specific movements to prepare the body for training or competi-tion. The coach should develop dynamic flexibility programs by analyzing soccer movements and then create stretches that improve flexibility and balance based on those movements. This is also a good time to reinforce the correct mechanics of running and to teach the body to move correctly. We want players to become stretched, warmed and educated at the same time and so allowing them just to jog and statically stretch seems a lost opportunity when time is so valuable.

STAGE TWO - Improved running technique

In the second part of the warm up session, it is time to speed things up. The coach needs to introduce quicker firing of the nervous system, so the drills must now promote fast arm and leg movement. This again can be accompanied by specific soccer techniques, so a 10 meter sprint can be preceded by a turn, lateral shuffle, backward shuffle, jump or volley. For more experienced players, these soccer techniques can be added to the middle or end of a sprint. All the time, the coach should be preparing his players to run fast. Remember - we cannot run fast by training slow.

STAGE THREE - Specific warm up

After three minutes of speed work, a ball should be introduced so that players get a feel for it, particularly before a game. This work can be passive to start with (players pass randomly in the penalty area), but should progress to active opposition, since game action speed is the most complex problem for a player to deal with. The aim, once again, is to speed up the nervous system, which in turn will improve anticipation, decision-making, perception and reaction speed. This type of warm up should thoroughly prepare a player for the demands of a game and should certainly give a team an edge.

Stage One:
Dynamic Flexibility

THE EXERCISES

The following exercises are classified as "dynamic stretches" or "flexibility runs". They encourage correct running technique and movement patterns and help to eliminate wasted motions. The coach needs to ensure that correct footwork becomes second nature, particularly for young players, so it is important that the exercises are carried out regularly and performed correctly.

It is best to commence dynamic flexibility exercises working 'on the spot' or 'in place', in order to groove the correct technique, before changing to the moving mode. This is particularly important for the younger player. The exercises must not be performed in an unthinking way; the coach must ensure that positive learning takes place.

As dynamic flexibility is based on soccer movements, the following exercises are by no means an all - inclusive list of stretches that can be used. These are only limited by the creativity of those designing the training program.

WARM UP WITHOUT THE BALL

The Format

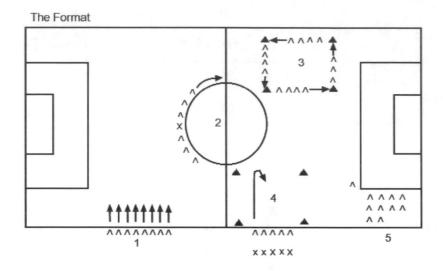

1   Players work across the pitch.
2   Players work around the center circle, the direction indicated by the coach.
3   Players work around a square, marked by four cones. Two sides work, while the other sides jog to recover.
4   Players work backwards and forwards across a rectangle, marked by four cones. The width is approximately 20 meters. One player works while the other rests.
5   Players work in a limited space, such as the center circle, penalty area or space between the penalty area and touch line and are free to move where they like. The set up in 3 or 4 could also be used for this method. Once the dynamic flexibility exercises are known, this is the preferred format for warming up since it also involves the players in finding space, anticipation and decision making.

1 Lunge Walk

Clasp your hands behind your head and then step forward and drop into a lunge position. It is important that you do not allow the knee of the forward leg to move in front of the toes. The back knee should be just off the ground. The head is up, the back arched and the body leaning backwards slightly. Pause for a moment in the bottom position and then repeat with the opposite leg.
Purpose: This movement is related to tackling or reaching out to trap a ball that is far from the body.

2 Twisting Lunge Walk

Clasp your hands behind your head and then step forward and drop into a lunge position. As you drop into the lunge position, twist the upper body so that your right elbow touches the outside of your left

leg. Do not allow the knee of your forward leg to move in front of your toes. The back knee should be just off the ground. The head is up, the back arched and the body leaning back slightly. Pause for a moment in the bottom position, then repeat with the right leg, touching the outside of the leg with your left elbow.
Purpose: This movement is related to tackling or reaching out to trap a ball. It also improves the ability to turn and change direction quickly.

3   Reverse Lunge Walk

Clasp your hands behind your head and then step backwards and drop into a lunge position. Do not allow the knee of your forward leg to move in front of the toes. The back knee should be just off the ground. The head is up, the back arched and the body should be leaning slightly back. Pause for a moment in the bottom position, then repeat with the opposite leg, moving backwards all the time.
Purpose: This is similar to back pedaling or reaching back to make a tackle or win a ball.

4   Reverse Twisting Lunge Walk

Clasp your hands behind your head. Step backwards and drop into a lunge position. As you drop back, twist your upper body so that the right elbow touches the outside of your left leg. Make sure the knee of your forward leg is not in front of the toes. The back knee should be just off the ground. The head is up, the back arched and the body should be leaning back slightly. Pause for a moment in this position then repeat with the opposite leg, moving backwards all the time.
Purpose: This is similar to back pedaling or reaching back to make a tackle or win a ball. It is also important in twisting or change of direction movements.

5   Calf Stretch

Step forward and bend the front leg, but make sure the knee is not in front of the toes. The back leg remains straight, with the heel staying down and the foot pointing straight forward. Hold this position for a moment, then repeat with the opposite leg, progressing forward with each step.
Purpose: To stretch the calf and to prepare the body for jumping and sprinting movements.

6   Walking Knee Stretch

Step forward with the left leg and then, using your hands, bring the right knee to the chest. Hold this position for a moment, then step forward with the right leg and repeat the action with the left leg.
Purpose: To improve hamstring flexibility, which is important for sprinting and for improving the ability to control balls that arrive at knee or thigh height.

7   Butt Kick

Whilst jogging slowly, the player's thigh points to the ground as the heel kicks upwards to the backside. This is a short, fast motion that is aided by correct arm mechanics.
Purpose: To stretch the quadriceps and to ensure proper sprint technique

8   High Knee Butt Kick

The player keeps his back straight and leans forward slightly whilst jogging. The leg is raised to a position where the thigh is parallel to the ground and the heel touches the backside. This is a short, fast motion where the heel does not touch the ground.
Purpose: To warm the hips, develop a quick knee lift and improve the ability to control a ball on the thigh.

9   Butt Skips

Whilst skipping, the player's thigh almost reaches the parallel as the heel kicks upwards to touch the backside. This action is repeated as quickly as possible on the other leg.

Purpose: To warm the hips, develop a quick knee lift and improve coordination and rhythm.

10   Arm Circles

Whilst jogging, bring the elbows together and in front of the face. Keep the elbows together as you move them upwards. At the top of the movement, split the elbows and then try to bring them close together behind your back. They are then brought back together in front and the action is repeated.

Purpose: To stretch and loosen the shoulders and upper body in preparation for sprinting.

11   Skips with knees to the side

As the player skips forward, the knee moves up and out. When the foot is returned to the ground, the action is repeated on the other leg. It is important an upright position is maintained and that the movement is done quickly.

Purpose: To develop knee drive, warm up and stretch the inside of the thigh and speed up the feet.

12   Skips across body

As the player skips forward, the knee is brought up and across the body. When the foot is returned to the ground, the action is repeated with the opposite leg. It is important that an upright position is maintained and that the knee leads the movement across the body, not the foot.

Purpose: Develop knee drive and warm up and stretch the outside of the legs.

13   Sideways skipping

Whilst skipping, the leg is moved upwards to a position where the thigh is just below the parallel and the knee points slightly outward. As the leg comes down, it is brought to the side and the foot double strikes the ground. The other leg is moved upwards at the same time and repeats the action. Speed of movement is vital in this drill.
Purpose: To develop quick feet, muscular coordination and rhythm.

14   High knee skips

Whilst skipping, the leg is moved forwards to a position where the thigh is parallel to the ground and the knee is bent at 90 degrees. The speed of movement is fast since each foot strikes the ground twice (left, left followed by right, right and so on). Emphasize the lifting action of the swing leg and the drive action of the support leg.
Purpose: Practice of correct sprinting position, arm mechanics and upright posture and to warm and stretch the legs.

15   One Leg Skip

As the player moves forward, he drives the leading leg up to a position where the thigh is parallel to the ground, and does a low skip on the standing leg. This action is repeated, with the player driving the same leg forward whilst continuing to skip on the other leg.

Purpose: To develop knee drive, warm the hip flexors and speed up the feet.

16   Knee Straight and Across Body

As the player moves forward, he drives the leading leg up to a position where the thigh is parallel to the ground and does a low skip on the standing leg. When the foot is returned to the ground the knee of the other leg moves upwards and across the body. This combination is repeated for a set distance and then the leg movements are reversed.

Purpose: Develop coordination, knee drive and warm up and stretch the outside of the legs.

17   **Hurdler's Stretch**

Whilst jogging, the player lifts his right leg as if stepping over an imaginary hurdle. He takes a few more steps, then repeats the action on his left leg. The movement should be easy and graceful. *Purpose:* To create stronger and more flexible groin muscles and to improve the side volley.

18   Cross-over Step

The player moves sideways, with the lead leg staying close to the ground. The trailing leg is raised, so that the thigh is parallel to the ground and the knee is bent at 90 degrees. From this position, the leg is brought through and lands in line with the lead leg (it is

important that the foot does not land in front). This action is repeated several times before the lead leg is changed.
Purpose: To warm the groin and teach the body how to move from a sideways to a front position.

19   Trunk Turns

Whilst jogging slowly, the player gently turns to one side and then to the other, with both arms moving to the turning side.
Purpose: To warm and stretch the lower back and obliques.

20   Drop Steps

As the player skips backwards, the right leg is lifted and moved to the side and then behind the body, with the thigh parallel to the ground and the knee bent at 90 degrees. The foot is returned to the ground and the same action is repeated on the left leg.
Purpose: To develop knee lift and to stretch the groin and hip flexors.

21   Carioca

The player runs sideways and crosses the legs, with right over left, then left over right. The body should not be allowed to twist and rotate, and the hips should do the work instead. The arms can be used for balance.
Purpose: To stretch and strengthen the lower back.

22   Tapioca

This movement is the same as the carioca, but the player should
make as many steps as possible in a small area. The feet should
"pop" off the ground.
Purpose: To stretch and strengthen the lower back and to speed up
the feet.

23   Skipioca

This movement is the same as the carioca, but the player skips
instead. The foot reaches well behind and is then followed by the
knee being driven across in front.
Purpose: To stretch and strengthen the lower back and to improve
coordination.

24   Volleyoca

This movement is the same as the carioca but, after the right leg has
crossed over behind the left, it is then driven across in front, with a
volley-type action. Work for 20 meters with the right leg volleying,
then change legs.
Purpose: To stretch and strengthen the lower back and to improve
volleying technique.

25   High Knees

Whilst jogging, the player raises his leg to a position where the thigh is parallel to the ground and the knee is bent to a 90 degree angle. This action is repeated as quickly as possible, with the player remaining in an upright position during the run.
Purpose: To warm the hip flexors, improve the ability to control the ball on the thigh and to ensure correct running action.

26   Leg Extensions

Whilst jogging, the player lifts the knee towards the chest, then extends the leg straight out, as if stepping over a hurdle. The action is repeated quickly on the other leg. The coach should ensure that the player does not lean back but "runs tall".
Variation - the same action but the player skips instead.
Purpose: To warm and stretch the hamstrings

COMBINATIONS

Once the player becomes proficient at performing each movement, the exercises can be brought together and combined. For example, a player can perform a knee lift followed by a heel to butt on the right leg, then repeat the action on the left leg. The list of combinations is almost endless.

There are two main advantages of combining movements. First, it becomes a more soccer-specific way to train because in soccer the player does not perform the same movement in arepetitive manner. Second, it becomes a more time-efficient way to train since a larger number of muscle groups can be stretched and warmed when combining, instead of repeatedly performing the same stretch. I shall show you several combinations, but remember - the list is almost limitless. It is therefore down to the coach to use his imagination, see what is required, then analyze the movements to make sure that all the areas that need to be stretched and warmed are covered.

1   Skip to the front and side

Whilst skipping forward, the player lifts the right leg to a position where the thigh is parallel to the ground and the knee is bent at 90 degrees. The foot is then returned to the ground where a double strike takes place. The same leg is lifted and moved to the side, with the knee leading the movement. The foot is then returned to the ground and two skipping motions are repeated on the left leg.

2   Knee tuck to lunge walk

The player steps forward with the left leg and, using his hands, squeezes the right knee into the chest. He holds this position for a second, then drops into a lunge position, with the right leg leading. The back knee should just be off the floor. Pause for a count in the bottom position and then repeat with the left leg, progressing forward with each movement.

Variation - the same movements performed walking backwards

3   Backwards skip plus drop step

Whilst skipping backwards, the right leg is brought up to a position where the thigh is parallel to the ground and the knee is bent at 90 degrees. At the top of the skip the player should be up on his toes. The same action is then repeated on the left leg. As the left foot returns to the ground, the right foot is immediately lifted and moved to the side. When this foot returns to the ground, the same action is repeated on the other leg.

4   Skips with knees to the side and across the body

As the player skips forward, the knee moves up and out. When the foot is returned to the ground, the action is repeated on the opposite leg. On the next skip, the knee is brought up and across the body and, when the foot is returned to the ground, the action is repeated with the other leg.

Variation - the same movements performed skipping backwards.

5   Foot slaps

Whilst jogging, the player lifts his right foot and touches it with his left hand. This foot is then returned to the ground and the movement is repeated with his left foot and right hand. Once the left leg is returned to the ground, he lifts his right foot behind his left knee and touches it with his left hand, and repeats the same action with his left foot and right hand.

Variation - the same movements but performed whilst skipping. This is far more strenuous and much more difficult to coordinate.

6   High knee butt kick plus leg extensions

Whilst jogging, the right leg is raised to a position where the thigh is parallel to the ground and the heel touches the backside. The right foot is returned to the ground and the action is immediately repeated on the left leg. This is a short, fast motion, where the heel does not touch the ground. The right knee is then lifted towards the chest before being extended out straight, as if stepping over a hurdle. This action is then repeated on the left leg.

Variations   a) the same movements performed running backwards

b) the same movements performed skipping; this is
   much more difficult to coordinate.

7   Knee lift plus butt kick

Whilst jogging, the player drives his right leg up to a position where the thigh is parallel to the ground and the knee is bent at 90 degrees. The leg is returned to the ground and immediately the heel of the same leg is kicked upwards to the backside, with the knee pointing towards the ground. Both movements are performed at speed. As soon as the right foot is returned to the ground, the same action is repeated on the left leg.

8   Calf stretch to walking knee stretch

The player steps forward on the left leg, making sure the knee is not in front of the toes. The back leg remains straight, with the heel staying down, sole flat on the floor and the foot pointing straightforward. He holds the position for a moment then, using his hands, brings his right knee to his chest. He pauses in this position, then steps forward on the right leg and carries out calf and knee stretches on the left leg.

9   Forward and backward skips

Whilst moving forward, the player performs three fast, low skips, concentrating on speed of the feet and knee drive. After the third skip, he rotates quickly and performs three fast backward skips. It is important that the player does not always turn the same way.

10   Skips plus arm circles

The player performs fast, low skips whilst circling his arms three times in a forward motion, then three times in a backwards motion. This is a very useful exercise for coordinating arms and feet.
Variations
a) the same movements performed skipping backwards;
b) the arms are held horizontal, with the hands touching and the elbows high. On the first skip, the arms are pulled apart, with the elbows moving behind the body, and on the second skip the hands are brought back together.

STRETCHES WITH PATTERS OR FAST FEET

At the end of the general warm up, the intensity must be increased and more soccer-specific exercises introduced. The

central nervous system needs to be stimulated in order that motor reactions are speeded up and there is a faster transmission of nerve impulses in order to improve coordination.

This can partly be achieved by combining FAST FEET or PATTERS with specific soccer techniques. Patters consist of rapid movements of the feet, taking tiny steps during which the full range of movements at the ankle is exaggerated. The knees are kept low, there is no heel contact with the ground and the leg speed is high. The body leans slightly forward, with shoulders relaxed and chin tucked in.

The player performs five rapid patters, then carries out the designated technique in a controlled manner. He does five more patters, then repeats the technique with the other foot. By using an odd number of patters, this should always bring the player onto his correct foot.

1   Patters plus pass with the inside of the foot

The player performs five quick patters, then passes an imaginary ball with the inside of the right foot. The kicking foot should be pointed outward at a right angle, with the heel down and toes pointing up. The right foot is then brought to the ground, five more patters are performed and the inside of the foot pass is repeated with the left leg.

The exercises that follow all have a similar format i.e. a practice of a movement or technique, alternating with five patters.

2   Patters plus pass with the instep

Patters followed by an imaginary pass with the right instep (laces). The foot is extended and the toes point downwards. After the kick, the foot follows through, swinging forwards and upwards. The right arm should be directly behind the body for balance. After the patters, the action is repeated on the left leg.

3   Patters plus pass with the outside of the foot

Patters followed by an imaginary pass with the outside of the right foot. The kicking foot should be pointed down and towards the inside of the player, with the ankle locked. The follow - through should have the kicking leg come across the body. After the patters, the action is repeated on the left leg.

4   Patters plus inside of the foot volley

Patters followed by an imaginary volley with the inside of the right foot. The leg is lifted and opened up, with the knee locked, foot at a right angle and the lower leg stiff. The follow through should be short, with the body leaning back slightly. After the patters, the action is repeated on the left leg.

5   Patters plus instep volley across the line

Patters plus an imaginary volley across the line using the right instep. The player plants and pivots on the standing leg and the left shoulder falls away, in order to allow the kicking leg to swing smoothly across the body. The kicking action is initiated from the hip. After the patters the action is repeated on the left leg.

6   Patters plus aerial control with the inside of the foot

Patters plus imaginary control of an aerial ball, with the inside of the right foot. The controlling leg is lifted and turned out from the hip. The foot is then withdrawn slowly from this position, with the ankle joint locked and the arms out to the side for balance. After the patters, the action is repeated on the left leg.

7   Patters plus aerial control with the instep

The player moves into and underneath the line of an imaginary ball. The right leg is then raised from the hip, with the toe pointing away, ankle relaxed and the knee bent slightly. The controlling leg descends quickly at first, then slows as it gets nearer the ground, as if trying to take the pace off the ball. After the patters, the action is repeated on the leftleg.

8   Patters plus outside of the foot volley

Patters followed by an imaginary volley strike with the outside of the right foot. The kicking action starts with raising of the knee from the hip of the kicking foot. The knee should be brought across the thigh of the non-kicking leg. The leg is then straightened as imaginary contact is made with the outside of the foot. The higher the volley, the more necessary it becomes for the non-kicking foot to leave the ground. After the patters, the outside of the foot volley is repeated on the left leg.

9   Patters plus heading

Patters followed by a two-footed take-off to head an imaginary ball. The feet are planted 8 - 10 inches apart, the arms are flung backwards and the upper body leans forward. The arms are then swung forward and upward, with the legs straightening and the feet pushing off the ground. The upper body moves backwards and then forwards to allow the forehead to meet an imaginary ball. The player should land on two feet and then repeat the action after five patters.

10   Patters plus step and pick up

The player steps forward with the left leg and drops into a lunge position. The back leg remains straight and stretched out behind him. From this position he scoops up an imaginary ball with his right hand. After the patters, he then repeats the action with opposite hand and leg.

11   Patters plus straight leg kick

The player brings his right leg up straight and kicks both hands, which have been stretched out in front. After five patters, he repeats the action on his left leg. It is important that he brings leg to hands and not hands to leg. He must therefore keep his back straight and raise the leg so that it reaches the horizontal.

12   Patters plus side leg raises

The player brings his right leg up straight and to the side, with toes pointing up. He must start as low as he feels comfortable and should only slowly increase the height at which the leg is raised. After five patters, the action is repeated on the left leg.

Forward, backward and sideways patters plus techniques

All the above exercises with patters can also take place in a one meter square.

```
2  .....................  1
:                        :
:                        :
3  .....................  4
```

   For example, the player starts at position 1 and performs an imaginary pass with the inside of the right foot. He then patters sideways to position 2 where he passes with the inside of the left foot. He patters backwards to position 3 where he again makes an imaginary pass with the inside of his left foot. Finally he patters sideways to position 4 and passes with the inside of his right foot before returning to position 1, with forward patters.

RHYTHMIC DYNAMIC FLEXIBILITY EXERCISES

Dynamic flexibility exercises can also be performed rhythmically, which makes the warm up more interesting as well as providing a great opportunity to work on players' timing and coordination. This can also help build team unity and promote communication amongst the players.

All the earlier exercises may be used and additional combinations of running steps and clapping in unison can enhance this section and make it fun. Better still, to make the warm up more enjoyable, why not use music? This will ensure that players are on the balls of their feet.

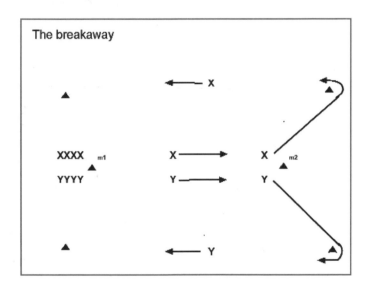

1   Six cones are placed as in the diagram, with the two central cones (M1 and M2) approximately 20 meters apart.

2   The players line up in pairs and in two lines, either side of M1

3   The first pair start together and do the same movement, in unison, down the centre lane.

4   The whole group follows down the central lane, using the same movement and with each pair working together.

5 When they reach M2, the pairs break away and jog down their sidelines.

6 The movement down the centre lane could include running sideways, backwards, butt kicks, high knees, skipping, drop steps, carioca etc, as well as combinations of running or skipping and clapping in time. The coach will inform the leading pair what the movement is going to be.

7 It is important to keep the players moving throughout the entire activity. Once the first pair has reached a third of the way down the centre lane, the next pair should start.

The breakaway with patters

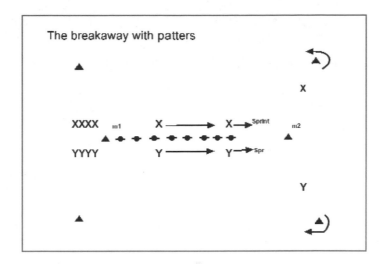

1   Six cones are placed as in the diagram, with the two central cones (M1 and M2) approximately 15 meters apart. Between M1 and M2 eight disc cones are placed on the ground, one meter apart.

2   The players line up in pairs and in two lines either side of M1.

3   The first pair start together and do five patters to the first disc cone, where they perform a given technique.

4   This pattern is repeated between each disc cone, at the end of which the players sprint to M2, then jog the rest of the course as shown.

5   Each pair must decide the starting foot, to ensure that the task can be completed in unison.

6   The movement down the centre lane could include patters with passes, volleys, headers, etc. The coach will tell the leading pair what the movement should be.

7   Once the first pair has reached the third disc cone,
         the next pair should start.

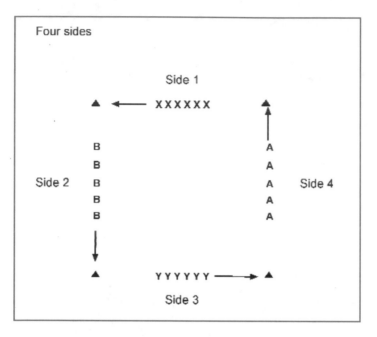

1   An area 20 meters by 20 meters is marked out with
         four cones.
2   The players are divided into four groups, with one
         group on each side of the square.
3   Players on sides 1 and 3 perform dynamic flexibility
         exercises in unison; players on sides 2 and 4 jog.
4   The leading player chooses the exercise and the rest
         of the group copy the exact movement.
5   At the end of each lap, the leading player drops to the
         back and the next player takes the lead.
6   All the usual dynamic flexibility exercises can be
         incorporated in this warm up, including skipping and
         clapping in time.

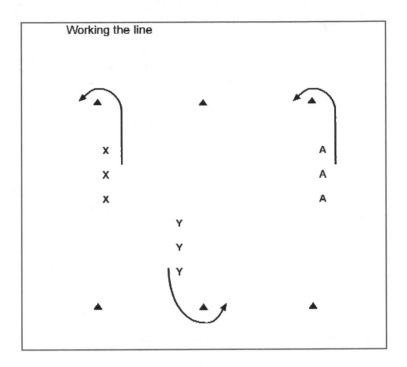

Working the line

1   Cones are laid out 20 meters apart.
2   Players are divided into groups of three, with each group assigned two cones.
3   The coach chooses the exercise and the players carry out his instructions.
4   The groups move around their two cones, copying the exact movements of the leading player.
5   Every so often, the leading player drops to the back and the next player takes the lead.
6   All the usual dynamic flexibility exercises can be employed in this warm up.

Variations
i)   The leading player chooses the exercise.
ii)   Instead of working around two cones, each group uses the lines of the soccer pitch.

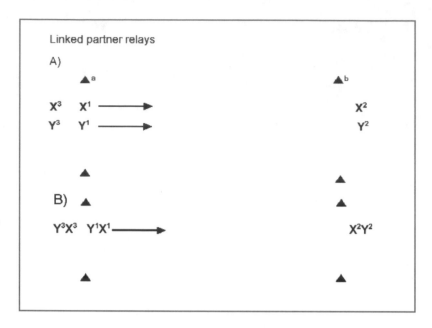

Linked partner relays

A)

X^3 X^1 ⟶

Y^3 Y^1 ⟶

B)

Y^3X^3 Y^1X^1 ⟶ X^2Y^2

1   Teams of six, divided into three pairs, with two pairs at line A and one pair at line B.

2   The first pair at line A link arms and perform, in unison, the dynamic flexibility exercise designated by the coach.

3   When they reach line B, the next pair link arms and perform the same exercise back to line A.

4   If the coach wants the players to perform cariocas, crossover steps etc, then the pair must turn sideways, with arms linked, and mirror each other's movements, as in diagram B.

5   To make the warm up more fun and more difficult, jumps to head a ball, full orientation, steps backwards and lateral movements can all be added to develop rhythm, timing and coordination.

Variation
The same movements but with pairs holding a rope.

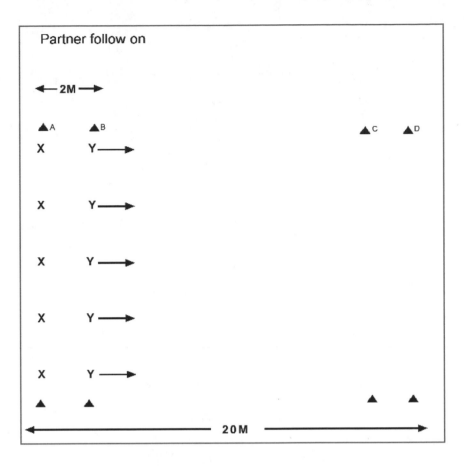

Partner follow on

←— 2M —→

1   Eight cones are set up as in the diagram.
2   Players work in pairs, with Xs starting on line A and Ys on line B.
3   Ys work to line D, performing the dynamic flexibility exercise designated by the coach.
4   Xs follow their partner and copy the exact movement until they reach line C.
5   On the way back, Xs lead to line A and Ys copy the same movement back to line B.
6   The usual dynamic flexibility exercises should be employed, including running, skipping, and clapping in unison.

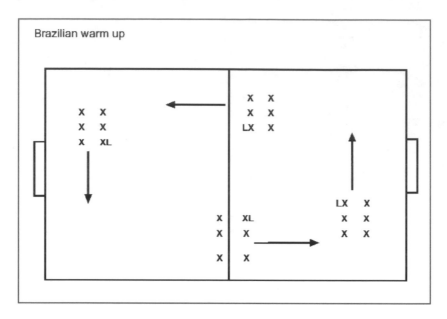

Brazilian warm up

1   Players work in groups of 6 - 18 ideally and move around the pitch in formation.
2   The front left player is always the leader and he chooses the dynamic flexibility exercise to be performed.
3   The rest of the group attempt to work in unison with him.
4   As the group reaches the end line or side line, the leader shouts "change" and all players turn 90 degrees. If done correctly, the two groups of three become three groups of two.
5   A new leader is now in position and he chooses the next exercise, which the rest of the group attempt to copy.
6   Additional running or skipping exercises, with rhythmic clapping, are useful for cooperation, timing and coordination.

Stage Two:
Improved Running for Better Soccer

All coaches agree that international soccer is getting faster. This means that players have even less time to adjust to situations and act on them. Improvement in modern defensive systems also brings a reduction in time and space, as opposition pressure increases. To overcome this players will have to sprint faster, stop more quickly under control and change direction more often in order to find space to receive passes. Speed and proper running techniques will become even more vital if success in soccer is to be achieved.

Coaches should therefore be aware of the need for systematic running and coordination training, since young players are often underdeveloped in this area and many never master good sprint mechanics. Basic competence for soccer should involve a whole variety of running movements, which demand changes in speed, direction, body gravity and frequency and length of stride.

To start with, however, players must be taught the basic mechanics of acceleration, deceleration and lateral movement. Once these have been mastered, they should be reinforced within the warm up, the second part of which should consist of pattern running workouts that involve planting, cutting, orientation, stopping and starting from different positions similar to those in a game. The drills should be carried out at maximum effort, so plenty of recovery time should be allowed between runs.

THE MECHANICS OF ACCELERATION, DECELERATION AND LATERAL MOVEMENT

Acceleration

Soccer is a game of 2 - 20 meter bursts and so a soccer player rarely reaches top speed. Acceleration is therefore the most important part of running in soccer and is largely determined by the strength of the first step. This step requires the greatest muscle power, the second a little less and so on, up to the fifth step. At this point the player should be reaching optimum speed.

Learning to lean correctly at the start of a sprint is also vital for soccer players. As the player builds up speed, the body should be in a deep lean in order to overcome gravity. On the first step it should be possible to draw a straight line from the ankle of the supporting leg, through the knee, hip, torso, shoulder and ear. At this point the centre of gravity should be ahead of the ground contact point, although by the third step the centre of gravity should be moving behind the ground contact point. Starting/accelerating is therefore a pushing, extending action.

Equally important to enable a player to accelerate is the length of the first five strides. Too often a player takes strides that are of almost equal length, with the first step nearly as long as the fifth. A long first step creates a "negative" shin angle, which blocks forward movement instead of assisting it, and makes full extension from the hip impossible. Players must learn to take a short first step and then progressively longer steps, in order to gain speed quickly. As with a car, it is important to go through the gears and not neglect gears one to four.

Starting Exercises For Acceleration

1   **Players work in pairs**. The working player leans into his
       partner, who extends his hands and holds his shoulders.
       From a 45 degree angle, the worker drives forward, while his
       partner back pedals for 10 meters. The support player then
       turns to one side and lets go and the working player sprints
       for 10 meters.

2   **Players pairs**. The working player falls forward and is
       caught by his partner. The latter immediately lets go, allowing
       the worker to sprint 10 meters.

3   **Lean, fall and run**. The player leans forward, with his body
       straight, until he reaches a point where he must step forward
       to catch himself. At this point he sprints.

4   **Arm action for acceleration**. The player either stands or
       sits, then practices a shorter, but more piston-like arm action,
       as quickly as possible. The lower body remains stationary.

5   **The acceleration ladder**. It is vital to create a 'pattern' for the
       first five steps, so that the correct movement sequence
       becomes automatic. The acceleration ladder is an excellent
       tool for training this and can be made from five agility poles,
       each 24 inches long. The distances, as recommended by
       Gary Winkler, head women's track coach at the University of
       Illinois are; 12 inches from the leading edge of the first rung
       to the leading edge of the second; 18 inches between the

second and third rungs; 24 inches between the third and fourth; 30 inches between the fourth and fifth. These distances can be adapted to the age and size of the players involved. The starting position should be one shoe length away from the first rung of the ladder.

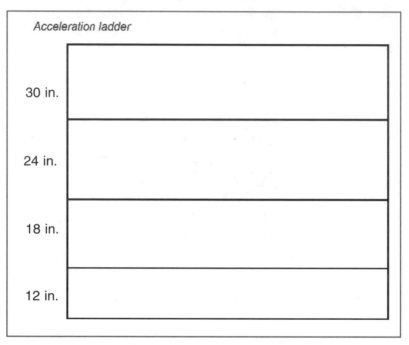

Acceleration ladder

30 in.

24 in.

18 in.

12 in.

The previous exercises helps create the correct mechanics for the first five steps. However, once the pattern has been established, functional soccer movements should be employed prior to the five steps, in order to make the exercises realistic. These could include jumps to head a ball, volleys, half turns, lateral steps and so on.

Deceleration

Almost as important as acceleration is deceleration, since being able to stop under control and change direction is an essential part of soccer. Also, stopping is where most injuries occur, since the high forces are mainly an eccentric muscle action (a very good reason for not statically stretching prior to playing or training, since this weakens eccentric muscle strength). In addition, it is during deceleration that most technical errors occur, which is another good reason for training this component correctly.

To decelerate and stop effectively, the mechanics must be understood. Unlike acceleration, which involves extending the hip, knee and ankle to produce force, stopping is the opposite. It is essential to bend the hip, knee and ankle, in order to reduce force, allowing the muscles that cross these three joints to act as shock absorbers. The stronger these muscles are eccentrically, the quicker a player will be able to stop and the less likely he is to get injured.

Exercises for Deceleration

1   **From a running start,** the player stops every five steps, for 50 meters. The stopping position must be held for a count of two.

2   **Stop on command**. The coach gives a verbal command to stop and start, with the player attempting to stop on alternate legs. Work for 50 meters.

3   **Stop on Reaction**. The coach gives a visual sign to stop and start, pointing in different directions to bring about a change of direction.

4

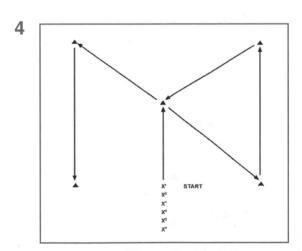

a)   Five cones are laid out as in the diagram. It is 7 meters from the start to the middle marker.

b)   X1 starts and follows the course shown.

c)   He stops at each cone, with feet parallel and ankles, knees and hips bent and freezes for a count of two.

d)   As soon as X1 leaves the middle cone, X2 starts.

Variations
i)   Stop at each cone in a staggered position, with left foot forward and right foot back.
ii)   Stop at each cone with right foot forward and left foot back.
iii)   Perform a header at each cone, land in a controlled manner and pause.
iv)   Work to the left after leaving the middle cone.

5

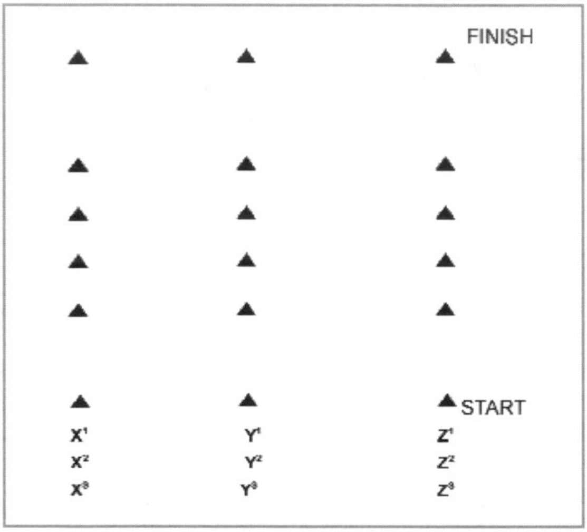

a)   12 cones are laid out as in the diagram, with 4 meters between each cone, 10 meters between the start and the first cone and 10 meters between the last cone and the finish.
b)   X1, Y1 and Z1 start at the same time, sprint to the cone in front of them and stop, with feet parallel and ankles, knees and hips bent. This position is held for a count of two.
c)   The same action is repeated at the next three cones, before players sprint to the finish.
d)   As soon as X1, Y1 and Z1 leave the first cone, X2, Y2 and Z2 start.
e)   Players wait at the finish and when they have all completed the task, the action is repeated in the opposite direction.

Variations

i)   Stop at each cone, in a staggered position, with left foot
      forward and right foot back.

ii)   Stop at each cone, with right foot forward and left foot back.

iii) Stop at each cone, in a staggered position, but alternate the
      front foot each time.

iv)   Stop at each cone, with left foot forward and right foot back.
      Pause, jockey back 3 steps to the right, then sprint to the next
      cone.

v)   Stop at each cone, with right foot forward and left foot back.
      Pause, jockey back 3 steps to the left, then sprint to the next
      cone.

vi)   Stop at each cone, with feet parallel and legs bent. Pause,
      and then jockey back 3 steps to the right and 3 to the left.

Lateral Movement

Soccer is a game played in short bursts, combined with sudden changes of direction and quick stops and starts. Whatever position you play, lateral mobility is critical to offensive and defensive soccer. Unfortunately many programs concentrate on starting ability, but fail to address the problem of lateral movement. Stopping quickly under control, then changing direction, is an area that must be trained.

The technique for lateral movement first requires the player to stop, then move off in another direction. Just before stopping, the player leans away from the direction of movement and lengthens the last few strides. The last step is the most important and must be the longest. Just as in deceleration, the ankles, knees and hips are bent, which lowers the centre of gravity and allows the muscles to act as shock absorbers. When the forward body movements have been successfully blocked, then the start technique is used for the change of direction. The first step must be taken in the intended direction.

Exercises for Lateral Movement

1   Run-Carioca-Run-Turn

The carioca agility drill is a cross stepping that propels the body laterally. The player runs five steps, breaks into a carioca for five steps before turning and repeating in the opposite direction. Start slowly, but once the action has been learned, perform it at speed, without slowing down in the transition from running straight to the carioca.

2   Run-Shuffle-Run-Turn

The shuffle agility drill is a side lateral movement and the procedure is the same as the run-carioca-run, except the player breaks into a shuffle. Run five steps, shuffle for five steps, then run five steps before turning and repeating the action in the opposite direction. Push off the balls of the feet, keep an equal distance between each shuffle and make sure the feet don't come together or cross.

3   Run-Back pedal-Run-Turn

The back pedal agility drill is a backward body movement sprint and the procedure is the same as the previous two drills. Run five steps, turn and run backwards for five steps, then run for five steps, turn and repeat in the opposite direction. As it is not possible to run straight and turn immediately into a backward pedal, the player must first do one carioca step before going into a back pedal. The hips lead the backward movement and the player rotates off the balls of the feet. Every time the drill is executed, make sure players turn both right and left.

4   Run-carioca-run-turn. Run-shuffle-run-turn. Run-back pedal-run-turn. This is merely a combination of the first three drills.

ADDITIONAL EXERCISES
For more advanced players, the task could be made more difficult by adding an extra activity between the run and the agility. This could be a header, volley, forward roll, backward roll or sit down eg a run, header and carioca or a run, forward roll and shuffle.

5   The Box

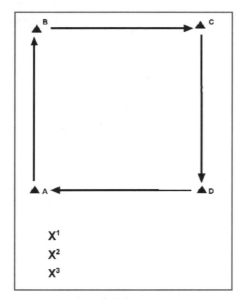

a)   4 cones are set up, 10 meters apart, to form a square.
b)   The players line up 6 meters from the first cone.
c)   X1 starts, jogs to cone A, then sprints to cone B.
d)   At cone B he shuffles sideways to cone C, facing out of the square.
e)   At cone C he runs backwards to cone D, then shuffles side ways to cone A, facing into the square. After finishing at cone A, X1 moves to the back of the group.
f)   X2 begins once X1 has started his first sprint.

Variations

i)   Players carioca between cones B and C and D and A.
ii)   Players sprint round the outside of the square, cutting hard at each cone with the left foot, then stepping in the direction of the next cone with the right foot.
iii)   Players sprint round the inside of the square, cutting hard at each cone with the left foot, then stepping in the direction of the next cone with the right foot.
iv)   Players work the opposite way round the square i.e. starts at cone D.

6   The Zig-Zag

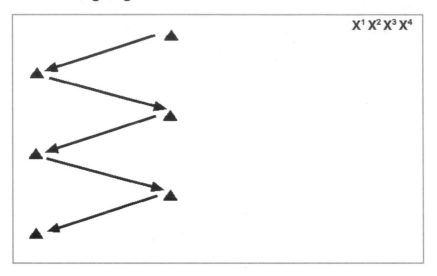

X¹ X² X³ X⁴

a)   7 cones are laid out as in the diagram. The distance between each cone is 4 meters.

b)   X1 starts, jogs to cone1, and then sprints the course shown.

c)   Once X1 has reached cone1, X2 starts.

d)   When everybody has completed the course, the process starts again.

e)   Emphasize fast foot plant and cut. Look out for players who cut better off one foot than the other.

Variations

i)   Run backwards from cone1.

ii)   Run sideways through the zig-zag, right foot leading.

iii)   Run sideways through the zig-zag, left foot leading.

iv)   Run sideways through the zig-zag, but change lead leg at each cone.

v)   Spin behind cones 2,3,4 and 5.

vi)   Cut in front of cones 2,3,4 and 5.

vii)   Right foot volley over cone 2, left foot volley over cone3 and so on.

7   Tag Games

Once the correct mechanics of acceleration, deceleration and lateral movement have been leearned, they then have to be used in 'random agility' situations. Up to this point the player has learned the pattern and sequence required, so knows what is to come. Random agility involves using visual and aural cues, from which the player has to make rapid decisions. This is close to the 'chaos of soccer', in which the player has to adapt to ever changing situations. Tag games are one of the best ways of creating random agility.

STAGE TWO (CONTINUED)

Once the correct mechanics of acceleration, deceleration and lateral speed have been taught, then these components must be joined together in the second part of the warm up. I have therefore devised a program of coordination exercises combined with sprints and stops and turns, which will ensure that the nervous system is stimulated and that the player is constantly forced to change his centre of gravity.

In the pre match warm up, this section should last no longer than four minutes, with the players ensuring that they take adequate rest between sprints. Prior to training, this section can last for up to ten minutes, depending on what is to follow and what the coach's priorities are. Once again there should be adequate rest intervals between sprints, since the exercises must be performed at maximum speed.

The running drills should be used as a link between dynamic flexibility exercises and the specific part of the warm up, but must not be performed in an unthinking way. It is the duty of the coach to see that this does not happen, since it is an important time for observation and instruction. Bad habits, which are detrimental to development, can be too easily LEARNED if left unchecked and not corrected. Younger players and players new to this material, will need
constant reminders of the correct biomechanical positions required during this part of the warm up. Once this has been achieved, progress should be made with players performing the drills without verbal cues.

The exercises themselves are divided into three categories - beginner level for under twelve's, intermediate level for under fifteen's and advanced level for players over fifteen. This arrangement however, needs to be fairly fluid, to take into account the ability levels of the individual players involved, particularly when players are using the material for the first time.

FIELD SET UP FOR BEGINNERS AND INTERMEDIATES

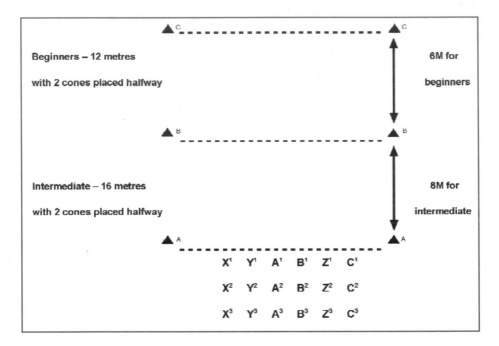

Co-ordination and running exercises for the beginner

Players start with feet parallel and shoulder width apart. It is important that when players are at line A or line C, they take up this stance before starting the sprint.

1)   Sprint from line A to line C, turn, take up the correct stance and sprint back to line A.
2)   Sprint to line B, turn and run backwards to line C.
3)   Run backwards to line B, turn and sprint to line C.
4)   Sprint to line B, turn and run sideways to line C.
5)   Run sideways to line B, turn and sprint to line C.
6)   Sprint to line B, carioca to line C
7)   Carioca to line B, sprint to line C.
8)   Sprint to line B, half turn, sprint to line C.
9)   Sprint to line B, 360° turn, sprint to line C.

10)   Run backwards to line B, 360° turn, run backwards to line C.
11)   Run sideways to line C, 360° turn, run sideways to line C.
12)   Sprint to line B, stop with feet parallel for the count of two
        then sprint to line C and repeat the stopping action.
13)   Sprint to line B, stop with left foot forward and right foot back
        for a count of two, then sprint to line C and repeat,
14)   Sprint to line B, stop with right foot forward and left foot back
        for a count of two, then sprint to line C and repeat.

All of the above exercises can be repeated but from different starting
positions:
◆   Left foot forward, right foot back
◆   Right foot forward, left foot back
◆   Back to the intended direction of movement
◆   Sideways to the intended direction of movement
◆   With a jump
◆   Step back
◆   Step to the side
◆   Two feet, one hand
◆   Half squat, back straight
◆   Walk to line A
◆   Jog to line A

It is important that the players adopt the above positions before
starting the sprint.

Coordination and Running Exercises for Intermediate Players

Players start with feet parallel and shoulder width apart. It is
important that when players are on line A or C, they take up this
stance before starting the sprint.

1)   Half turn then sprint to line C. At line C take up the correct
       stance, half turn and sprint to line A.
2)   Turn 360° sprint to line C.
3)   Sprint to line C and turn 360°.
4)   Sprint to line B, turn 360° and sprint to line C.
5)   Move three steps to the right, sprint to line C.
6)   Move three steps to the left, sprint to line C.

7)   Move three steps to the right then three steps to the left, sprint to line C.

8)   Sprint to line C, move three steps to the right then three steps to the left.

9)   Sprint to line B, stop with feet parallel, pause for a count of two, then move three steps to the right, three to the left and sprint to line C.

10)   Move back three steps, sprint to line C.

11)   Sprint to line C, move back three steps.

12)   Sprint to line B, stop with feet parallel, and pause for a count of two then move back three steps and sprint to line C.

13)   Jockey back three steps to the right, sprint to line C.

14)   Jockey back three steps to the left and sprint to line C.

15)   Jockey back three steps to the right, three to the left and then sprint to line C.

16)   Sprint to line C, jockey back three steps to the right.

17)   Sprint to line C, jockey back three steps to the left.

18)   Sprint to line C, jockey back three steps to the right then three to the left.

19)   Sprint to line B, stop with feet parallel, pause for a count of two then jockey back three steps to the right, three to the left and sprint to line C.

20)   Jump to head ball, sprint to line C.

21)   Sprint to line C, jump to head the ball.

22)   Sprint to line B, stop with feet parallel, pause for a count of two, jump to head a ball and sprint to line C.

23)   Move back three steps, jump to head a ball then sprint to line C.

24)   Sprint to line C, move back three steps, jump to head a ball.

25)   Sprint to line B, stop with feet parallel, pause for a count of two, move back three steps, jump to head a ball, sprint to line C.

26)   Volley to the right, volley to the left, sprint to line C.

27)   Sprint to line C, volley to the right, volley to the left.

28)   Sprint to line B, stop with feet parallel, pause for a count of two, volley to the right, volley to the left then sprint to line C.

The number of co-ordination and sprint exercises are limitless. Once again it is down to the imagination of the coach. All of the above exercises can include starting or stopping on different feet, as well as beginning with a walk or a jog.

Coordination and Running Exercises for Advanced Players

Field Set Up

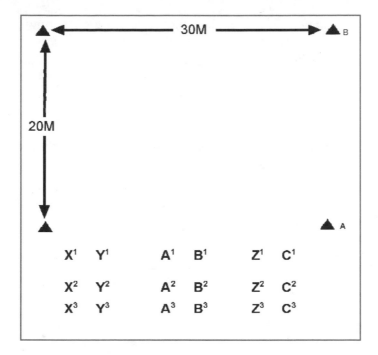

The pressure is increased by the players competing in pairs, as shown in the diagram. After racing to line B, the players jog back to the start.

1)   Start with feet parallel, sprint to line B.
2)   Start with left foot forward, right foot back.
3)   Start with right foot forward, left foot back.
4)   Face each other and sideways to direction of the sprint.
5)   Back to back but sideways to the direction of the sprint.
6)   Back to the direction of the sprint.
7)   Back to the direction of the sprint. Take off on both feet, jump and turn 180° in the air, land and sprint.
8)   Jump to head a ball.
9)   Back to direction of sprint, jump to head a ball.
10)   Jump and shoulder charge each other.
11)   Back to direction of the sprint, jump and charge each other.
12)   Start in prone position with hands placed near the shoulders.

13)   Start in press up position.
14)   Place ball at the end of the sprint zone. First to the ball wins.
15)   Sprint to line B and back to the start.
16)   Player 1 runs forward moving from side to side, whilst player
        2 runs backwards, responding to player 1's movements.

The coach can start the above exercises with a clap or a dropped
ball.

DEVELOPMENT

Using the same 30m by 20m grid, the players move anywhere they
like, but accelerate into space whenever they see it.

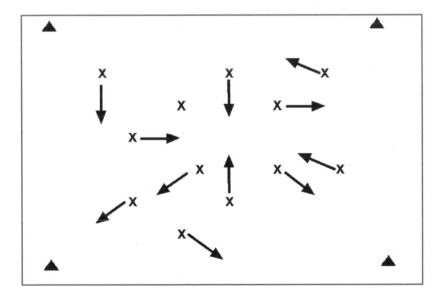

        Once the format has been established, then many of the
previous exercises from the beginner and intermediate sections may
be used; however it becomes more difficult since players have to be
aware of finding space and avoiding other people. This will involve
anticipation, decision making, reaction and perception, as well as
co-ordination due to the readjustment of the body, in order to reach
the first step quickly before sprinting.

        The coach should start off by directing the players in the com-
bination of movements he wants, but should quickly progress and

allow players to experiment with their own combination of exercises, particularly the standing up and moving starts. Once again the coach must observe the session carefully and be prepared to correct any mechanical errors that occur.

Additional Coordination and Running Exercises for All Ability Groups

1   Sequence Running

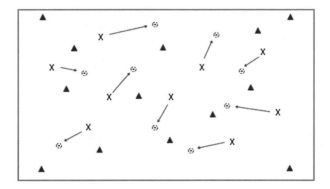

a)   Balls and cones are spread out over a quarter of a pitch.
b)   Players jog in and out of the cones and balls until the coach shouts out a sequence e.g. ball, cone.
c)   The player has to sprint and touch a ball and cone, with his hand and in that order.
d)   Once he has completed the sequence, he carries on jogging.
e)   Make sure that there is one ball and one cone for each player.

Variations (1)
i)   Lengthen the sequence e.g. ball, cone, cone, and ball.
i)   Run in sequence but toe touch the top of the ball and cone twice.
iii)   Run in sequence but touch ball and cone with both knees.
iv)   Run in sequence but volley over the top of ball and cone.
v)   Touch a cone, but dribble a ball 2 meters and return.
vi)   Jump to head a ball, then jockey back 3 steps at each cone and ball during the sequence.

vii)   Jump to head a ball and jockey back 3 steps before commencing the sequence.

viii)   Decelerate at each cone and ball during the sequence and pause for a count two.

Variation (2)
        Place different colored cones, at random, over quarter of a pitch. The coach shouts out a colored sequence e.g. red, yellow, blue and white and the player has to run and touch each in that order. All the variations from the previous exercise can be used for this practice.

2   Pass and move

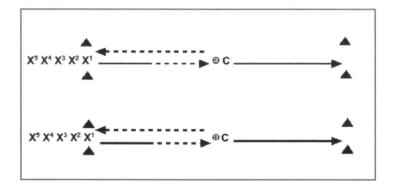

a)   Players line up in groups of five. X1 starts between two cones, which are one meter apart and five meters from the coach.

b)   The coach has a ball and faces X1.

c)   He passes to X1, who passes it back first time. X1 then sprints to the cones, which are five meters behind the feeder and waits there.

d)   As soon as X1 has sprinted, the coach passes to X2, who repeats the drill.

e)   When all players have completed the sprint, the action is repeated from the other end.

f)   The player's first touch must also be the first step of the run. He must therefore lean in the direction of the run at the moment of ball contact.

g)   Players must concentrate on acceleration and the drive from their first step.

Variations

> After passing the ball back to the coach, the player can:

i)   Jump to head an imaginary ball before sprinting.
ii)   Turn 360 degrees before sprinting.
iii)   Move backwards three steps before sprinting.
iv)   Touch the cones to their right and left before sprinting
v)   Move back three steps, jump to head a ball before sprinting
vi)   Volley right and left before sprinting.
vii)   Jump sideways over a cone before sprinting
viii)   Instead of passing the ball on the ground, the coach can throw balls for players to volley, head, chest and volley etc, before they start their sprint.

3   Shadow runs

a)   Players work in pairs, in a 30 meter square.
b)   B lines up within arms length of A and just behind the left or right shoulder.
c)   Player A moves anywhere he likes in the grid and B follows, imitating the changes in speed, movement and direction, whilst trying to maintain the same distance.
d)   Change roles after one minute.

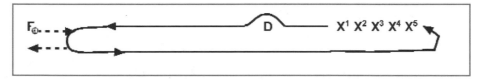

a)   Players line up in groups of five, with a feeder positioned with a ball, approximately 20 meters away.
b)   A passive defender stands facing the running group and about 5 meters away.
c)   X1 starts and sprints past the defender, who only offers token resistance.
d)   The feeder immediately plays a rolling ball towards X1, who returns the ball with a one touch pass, then turns and sprints to the back of the file. If the ball is played back with the right foot, then the player spins out to his left and if it is played back with the left foot then the player spins out to his right.

e)   Once X1 has returned to the back of the file, X2 starts.
f)   Work for two minutes then change the feeder and defender.
g)   Players should concentrate on acceleration, first touch and speed of turn.

Variations
A)   After passing the ball back to the feeder, the players:
      i)   Jump to head an imaginary ball, turn and sprint.
      ii)   Move back three steps, turn and sprint.
      iii) Move sideways three steps, turn and sprint.
      iv)   Jockey three steps, turn and sprint.

B)   Allow the defender to become more active.
C)   Make players start from different positions e.g. lying face down, sitting, lying on back, kneeling, press up position etc.

5   Movement Freedom

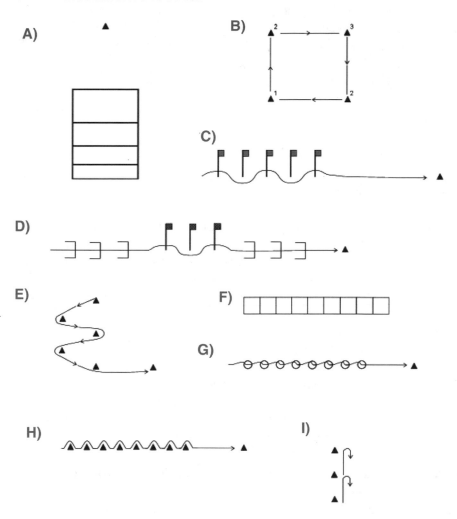

Equipment
1)   30 cones or disc cones.
2)   One acceleration ladder.
3)   One coordination ladder.
4)   8 hoops.
5)   6 hurdles.
6)   9 flag poles.

Formation
The equipment is set out on half a pitch.

Station Procedures

Station A   Fast run through the acceleration ladder plus 5 meter sprint

Station B   Set up 4 cones or markers, in an 8 meter square. Run forward from cone 1 to cone 2, sideways from cone 2 to cone 3, backwards from cone 3 to cone 4 and sideways from cone 4 to cone 1.

Station C   Set poles 18 inches apart. Run through poles with high, fast knees plus 5 meter sprint to cone.

Station D   Run over 3 hurdles, through 3 poles, over 3 more hurdles plus 5 meter sprint.

Station E   Set up 5 cones in a W shape and 4 meters apart. A further marker is placed 5 meters away. Run sideways through the W shape, changing lead leg at each cone plus 5 meter sprint to cone.

Station F   Coordination ladder. Single foot in each rung plus 5 meter sprint.

Station G   Set 8 hoops, 1 meter apart. Sprint through 8 hoops, putting one foot in each plus 5 meter sprint to cone.

Station H   Set cones 24 inches apart. Sprint over 8 cones, using one leg and keeping the other leg dead, plus sprint to end marker.

Station I   Place 3 cones in a straight line, 5 meters apart. Shuttle to the first cone and back, second cone and back.

Station J   Place 3 cones in a V shape, 4 meters apart. A further cone is placed 10 meters away. Start on the middle cone of the V. Run to the left cone, back to the middle,

right cone, back to the middle and then sprint to the
10 meter cone.

Players jog slowly around the area and are then free to use the
stations in any order. Maximum effort is required at each station,
along with correct technique. Players must make sure that they have
sufficiently recovered before using the next station.

Stage Three:
The Specific Warm Up

The specific part of the warm up now takes place, and this section should see the introduction of a ball. Games should be planned which not only continue to increase body temperature, but also enable players to rehearse the complex skills that are about to be performed. The neural aspects of the warm up, which are important in the first two sections, now become the major factor. Although the use of a ball is entertaining and motivating for most players, this section still has to be game-orientated, relevant and educational, with certain criteria being followed.

The main aim is to ensure that the brain and nervous system function more rapidly. Unfortunately, many warm up programs are simply not relevant to the game. Players stand still and pass, and are not required to make fast, accurate decisions, which happens once the game starts. As a result, players are not called upon to utilize their visual and auditory senses, which are needed to process the major elements of the game.

Passing, receiving and controlling the ball are inter-related skills and should form the major part of the ball work. However, it must be put in an environment which involves an awareness of space, time and other players. Many of the practices that follow this introduction may start with passes from the hand, since eye-hand coordination is quicker than eye feet. Not only is this good fun, it also speeds up the nervous system and creates a faster motor program. Once the pattern of the practice has been established and the movement speeded up, the ball can then be passed by feet.

Practices working both sides of the body also help to improve skill levels and produce greater coordination in the nervous system. Therefore during this phase of the warm up, the coach should insist that players jump off right and left feet when heading a ball, turn both ways, jockey to the right and left and pass with right and left feet. In fact, part of the warm up could be passing and receiving with left foot only, then right foot only.

For those players who have reached the AUTONOMOUS phase of the learning process (they are able to perform skills automatically, enabling them to concentrate on other aspects of the game, such as movement of other players and the options available), then their thought processes can be challenged by multi-tasking - getting them to perform more than one task at a time. For example, whilst passing and moving in a restricted area, the player has to perform an imaginary skill such as jumping for a header or volleying with the instep, just before receiving the ball. The use of different pin-nies can also improve colour vision, with the players passing in a sequence, such as red to blue, blue to green and green to red and with a specific foot, as designated by the coach. These types of warm up practice are good for those who have reached this level of learning and there is no place for 'slow thinking' activities, which have a negative effect on the brain and nervous system.

Another basic element often missing from the warm up is a combination of technical and tactical work. Players need to practice dribbling and crossing on the run, defensive and attacking heading, one touch finishes, overlaps etc and this should be done in areas of the field where they would actually take place in a game. In addition, players should work on programs that are more position specific, with the right full back, for example, working with the right midfield player, near the appropriate touchline.

Towards the end of this section of the warm up, we should expect the action to be played at match speed, with plenty of short sprints and changes of direction, in a game situation. To meet the speed related demands of the game, special rules should be applied, such as one or two touch play. This makes players practice at top speed, which in turn speeds up decision-making and reduces time on the ball. In addition, it also makes players address the issue of defensive play and pressing as a group - an aspect of play which many warm ups ignore.

Whatever happens, the coach must continually change this section of the warm up and always attempt to make it interesting and challenging. If players know what is coming each time, then it becomes difficult to keep them focused. We must try to keep the brain stimulated by putting on interesting, but relevant games that demand concentration, awareness, quick reactions, rapid decision-making and peripheral vision. I believe the following practices meet these demands.

1

1)   The players move around in a 30 meter by 20 meter grid. Four players start with a ball.

2)   Whilst moving they randomly pass the balls to each other.

3)   The players without balls should look for opportunities to call and ask for passes from those in possession.

4)   After passing the ball, the player should sprint out of the space, before looking for another ball.

5)   The player receiving the ball should try to take it off line with his first touch.

Variations
i)   Receive with the inside of the foot.
ii)   Receive with the outside of the foot.
iii)   Receive with the back foot, side on.
iv)   Two touch
v)   One touch
vi)   Dribble at pace before passing.

vii)   Dribble with take-overs.
viii)   Receive with the inside of the foot, pass with the outside.
ix)   Receive with the outside of the foot, pass with the inside.
x)   Players call out who they are going to pass to before they
        receive the ball.
xi)   Perform a trick before passing.
xii)   Receive and pass, right foot only.
xiii)   Receive and pass, left foot only.
xiv)   Dribble, turn and pass.

2

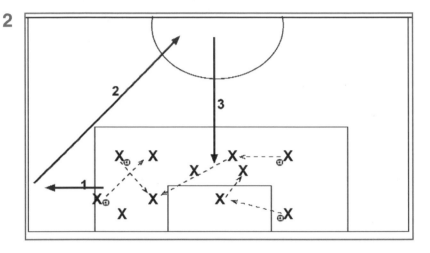

1)   The players move around in one penalty area, randomly
        passing balls to each other.

2)   On a signal from the coach, the players run to another area of
        the field and carry on passing.

3)   For example, on the first signal they run to the area between
        the touch line and the penalty box, on the next signal to the
        centre circle and then to the six yard box and so on.

4)   The players must remember to take the balls with them.

5)   All the variations used in exercise one may be used in this
        practice.

3

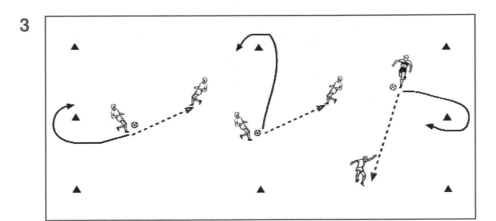

1) A grid 30 meters by 20 meters is set up, with any number of cones placed along the side.

2) The players move around the grid, passing the ball at random. There should be a minimum of 3 balls per 12 players.

3) After passing the ball, the player sprints to any cone on the side.

4) Here he does a two-footed jump from side to side, over the cone, then returns to passing in the grid.

5) All the passing variations used in exercise one can be repeated in this practice.

Variations at the cones

i) the player jumps backwards and forwards once over the cone before returning to the grid.

ii) hop on one leg over the cone.

iii) sit down at the cone.

iv) chest on the floor at the cone.

v) touch the cone with one hand and sprint back into the grid.

vi) take 3 steps backwards, turn and sprint back into the grid.

vii) jockey back 3 steps.

viii) decelerate at the cone, pause then sprint back into the grid.

ix) jump, 180° turn in the air, then sprint back into the grid.

x) jump to head an imaginary ball, then turn and sprint back into the grid.

xi)   spin behind the cone.
xii)   run round the cone backwards.

4

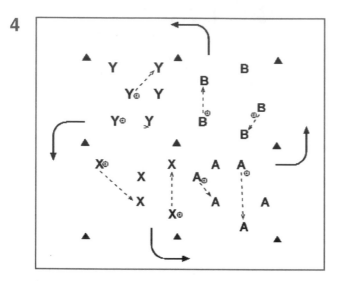

The above set up offers a pattern that can be adopted safely with large groups.

1)   9 cones are used to set up 4 grids, each 15 meters by 15 meters.

2)   5 to 8 players work in each grid, with 2 balls per group. If more players are involved, the grid can be made bigger and extra balls used.

3)   Players move around their area, passing the balls at random.

4)   On a signal from the coach, the players immediately leave their balls, move out from the front of the grid, as indicated by the arrows, then jog anti-clockwise around the complete square, before moving on to the next grid. Thus, players in grid one will move to grid two, those in grid two to grid three and so on.

5)   Here they resume passing at random.

6)   All the variations used in exercise one may be used in this exercise.

5

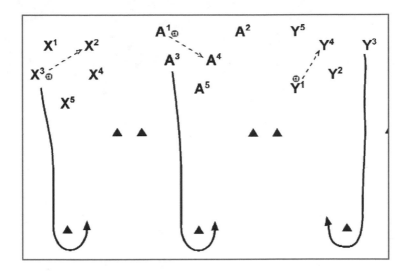

1)   Three squares are set up, each 15 meters by 15 meters. A cone is placed 15 meters from the square.

2)   The players are numbered from one to five, but pass the ball randomly amongst themselves.

3)   When the coach shouts out a number eg three, all those players with that number have to break from the grid and sprint around the cone placed in front of them.

4)   All the various ways of passing and receiving, as suggested in exercise one, can be used in this warm up.

Variations on the running section
i)   run backwards to the cone
ii)   run sideways
iii)   carioca
iv)   spin behind the cone
v)   cut back two steps at the cone
vi)   jump over the cone
vii)   complete a full turn on the way to the cone
viii)   call out two numbers and they have to race to the cone

6

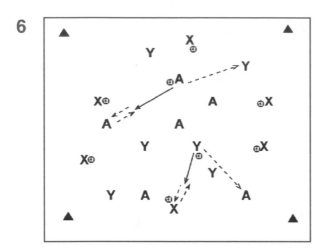

1)   A 20 meter square is marked out with 4 cones.

2)   3 groups of 6 players are organized in different pinnies.

3)   One group lines up around the outside of the grid, with a ball each.

4)   The two groups in the middle pass and move using two balls.

5)   After a player has passed the ball, he has to run to the outside, play a one/two with a wall player, then return to the inside of the square.

6)   After two minutes, change the outside group.

Variations
i)   two touch with the outside players.
ii)   volley back.
iii)   head back.
iv)   chest and volley.
v)   pass back to the outside player, then run around him.
vi)   toe touch four times on top of the ball, then pass back

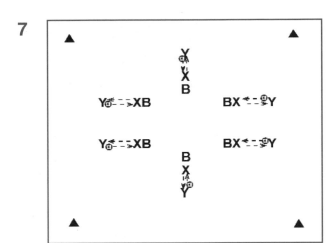

1) A 25 meter square is marked out with 4 cones.

2) Three groups of six players are organized in different colored pinnies.

3) One group lines up around the outside of the grid with a ball each.

4) In the middle, the players pair off with a player of another color.

5) B follows X, as X plays a one touch pass back to Y.

6) X and B turn immediately and B becomes the player looking for a one touch pass with Y. X tracks B closely.

Variations
Y throws the ball for the inside player to:
i) volley
ii) head
iii) chest and volley
iv) half-volley
v) control on the thigh

X becomes the attacker and B the defender. X plays a one/two with as many Y's as possible, which B tries to prevent. Work for 30 seconds, then X's change with the outside group.

8

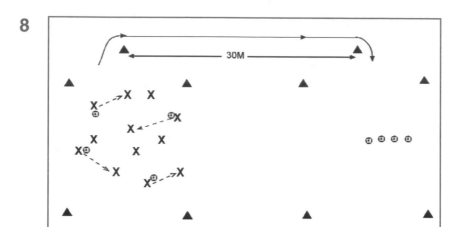

1)   Two grids, 25 meters by 25 meters, are set up parallel and approximately 20 meters apart.

2)   The players move around in one grid, passing the ball at random. There should be 4 balls for every 12 players.

3)   On a signal from the coach, the players leave their balls, run around the two outer cones and into the other grid.

4)   Here 4 balls are waiting and the players carry on passing and moving as before. On a signal from the coach, the players leave their balls, run around the two outer cones and return to the original grid.

5)   All the passing and receiving variations, used in exercise one, may be repeated in this exercise.

Variations
The players are split into two groups and operate in both grids. On a signal from the coach, they leave their balls, run around the two outer cones and into the other grid. Here they carry on moving and passing. Care must be taken when the two groups pass during the run.

9

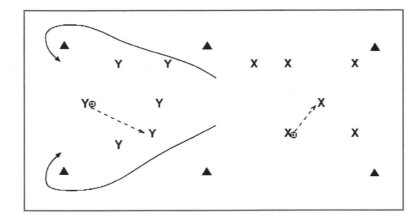

1) Two 20 meter grids are set up, as in the above diagram.

2) The players are divided into two groups and work in separate grids. One group wears a set of pinnies.

3) The players pass the ball at random within their group, but on a signal from the coach, sprint into the opposite grid.

4) Here they run around either of the end cones before going back to passing the ball.

5) Players must be careful not to bump into other players as they switch grids.

6) All the previous passing and receiving exercises may be used in this practice.

Variations
i) players run round either of the rear cones before sprinting into the other grid.
ii) players run round either of the rear cones, sprint into the other grid, run round either of the end cones, then carry on passing.
iii) players touch all six cones with their hand and in any order, before moving into the other grid.

10

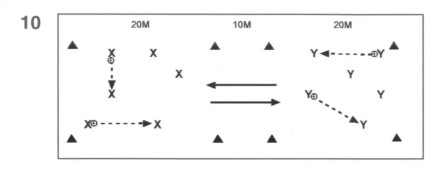

1)   Two 20 meter grids are set up, with a 10 meter zone in between.

2)   The players are divided into two groups and work in separate grids. One group wears a set of pinnies.

3)   The players pass the ball at random within their grid.

4)   On a signal from the coach, each team has to move into the other grid as quickly as possible.

5)   However, in the free zone, the players have to perform exercises as designated by the coach. These could include:
   a)   a sprint
   b)   a run backwards
   c)   a run sideways
   d)   carioca
   e)   a sprint with a full turn
   f)   a sprint with a half turn
   g)   two footed jumps
   h)   a hop
   i)   jump to head an imaginary ball
   j)   five quick steps and volley
   k)   sprint, stop, sprint

6)   Once in the other grid players resume passing the ball. All the passing variations used in Exercise One can be repeated in this practice

11

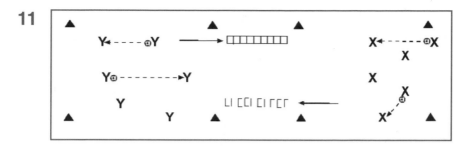

1) Two 20 meter grids are set up, with a 15 meter free zone in between. On one side of the zone, there is a coordination ladder and on the other 10 low hurdles, each 1 meter apart.

2) Players are divided into two groups and work in separate grids. One group wears a set of pinnies.

3) The players pass the ball at random within their grid. On a signal from the coach, each team has to move into the other grid. However, the group moving from left to right has to move down the coordination ladder first, whilst the group moving from right to left has to run over the hurdles.

4) Once in the other grid, players resume passing the ball.

5) All the passing and receiving exercises used in Exercise One may be performed in this exercise.

12

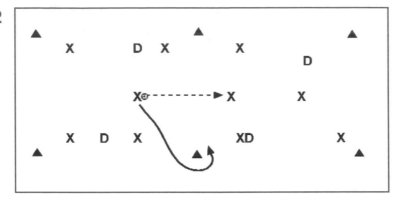

1)   A 30 meter by 20 meter grid is set up using 8 cones, as in the diagram.

2)   A keep ball game of 10 v 4 is played in the grid. The 10 attackers are only allowed two touches.

3)   Once the player has passed the ball, he sprints round one of the cones on the outside of the grid and then returns to the keep ball game.

4)   The attacker must look for a new position once he returns to the grid.

5)   If the defenders win the ball, they give it straight back to the attackers.

6)   Change the defenders every three minutes.

Variations
i)   Attackers are only allowed one touch.
ii) Attackers are allowed one or three touches.

13

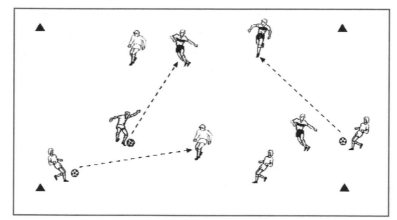

1)   The players form groups of three, with one ball per group.

2)   They pass and move over a quarter of a pitch, practicing various techniques and filling space.

3)   They gradually spread out more so that passes are longer and can be played with more pace.

4)   Care must be taken to avoid other groups.

Variations

i)   The player with the ball dribbles to a team-mate, plays a one/two, then makes a similar wall pass with the other member of the group. Play for one minute then a new player has the ball.

ii)   The player with the ball dribbles at pace to a team-mate, performs a takeover, then sprints out of the space. The new player repeats the exercise with the third member of the group.

iii)   The player with the ball dribbles at a moderate pace. The other two players move into space but maintain constant eye contact with Player one. After a few seconds, the player with the ball passes to another and the process starts again.

iv)   The player with the ball plays a wall pass, gets the return, and then immediately passes to the third player, who has to show for it quickly. The action is then repeated.

v)   One player has the ball, whilst the others serve as targets and move randomly throughout the area. The dribbler makes a 15 meter pass to one of the targets and then sprints to support the pass. He receives a short return ball, then has to locate and pass to the other target man. All passes should be a minimum of 15 meters. The person with the ball works for one minute and then players change roles.

vi)   Play 2 v 1 in a small area, but keep changing the defender.

4

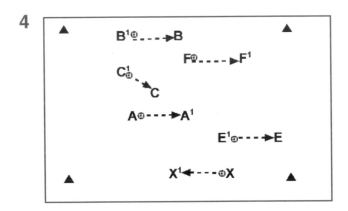

1)   The players work in pairs on half a pitch, with one ball between two.

2)   They pass and move, keeping about 10 meters apart.

3)   The coach then calls out various distances, from 2 meters to 30 meters and how many touches and the players have to respond accordingly, but always on the move.

4)   The players have to be aware of the quality and weight of the passes, as well as the quality of the first touch.

Variations
Every so often whilst passing, one player will dribble at speed towards the other and perform a take over.

i)   The player without the ball moves where he likes, whilst the player with the ball maintains constant eye contact with him. The player without the ball then checks away, sprints back, calls for the ball and roles are reversed.

ii)   A passes to A1, then jogs out of the space. A1 takes the ball
        on the half turn and touches it twice as he dribbles away. He
        then turns, passes to A, who repeats the movement.
iii)   1 v 1 for 20 seconds.

15

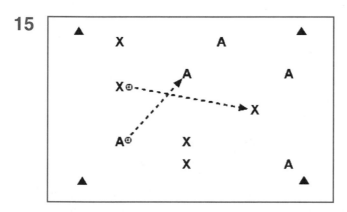

1)   Divide the players into groups of five, one ball per group.

2)   The players work on half a pitch and pass the ball in any
        direction. However, they cannot pass the ball back to the
        person who gave them the ball.

3)   Once the players have got the mood for passing quickly, then
        change the requirements.

4)   After five passes the player with the ball has to juggle it four
        times, then volley to another player. That pass must be
        controlled in the air before it is brought to the ground and the
        five passes start again.

5)   It is important that one player runs towards the juggler, whilst
        the rest make sharp runs away.

Variations
i)   increase or decrease the number of volleys.
ii)   knock up, then head to the next player.
iii)   volley with the inside of the foot.
iv)   volley with the thigh.
v)   volley with the outside of the foot.
vi)   half volley.

16

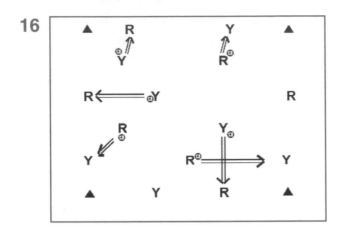

1)   Players line up in a 20 meter square, as in the diagram. A minimum of 14 players will be required for this exercise.

2)   Three yellows and three reds start with a ball in the middle, dribble to the sides, hand over to any of the players on the outside and take their place.

3)   Players receiving the ball have to dribble to any of the other three sides and hand over. They CANNOT dribble to players on the same side.

4)   Care must be taken to avoid other players.

Variations
i)   Red can only change with red, yellow can only change with yellow.
ii)   Red must change with yellow, yellow must change with red.
iii)   Players dribble half-way across the grid, then pass to a player on the outside.
iv)   Players dribble to the side, then just as they reach the player on the outside they pass a ball behind him, which he has to turn and chase.
v)   As in d), but when players have chased the ball, they turn, play a 1 - 2 with the player who gave them the ball, then dribble back to the middle.
vi)   The inside player passes to the outside player, who immediately passes it back. The outside player then takes two quick steps back and:

- jockeys to the right
- jockeys to the left
- jumps to head an imaginary ball
- volleys right and left, then takes the ball left by the dribbler

17

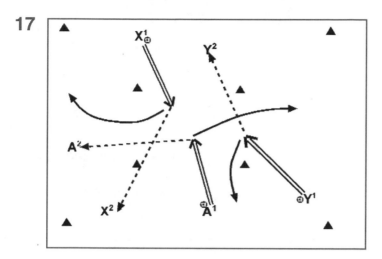

1) A 30 meter square is marked out with four cones. Inside this area, a 10 meter square is marked out.

2) Players work in pairs, one ball between two. The player with the ball dribbles at speed into the small square, turns and passes to his partner, who has moved into another area of the large square.

3) The player who has passed the ball sprints out of the middle square and looks for a space in the large square.

4) The player receiving the ball dribbles at speed into the smaller square, turns and passes to his partner, who has moved into another part of the large square.

Variations
i)   The player with the ball has to perform a trick in the small square before passing the ball.
ii) Players dribble using left foot only.
iii) Players dribble using right foot only.
iv) Players alternate each touch with the left and right feet.
v)   The dribbler has to keep constant eye contact with his partner.

18

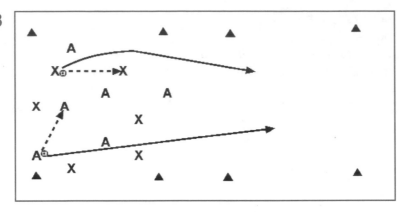

1)   Two 20 meter grids are set up, as in the above diagram.

2)   The players are divided into groups of five or six, with one group wearing pinnies. Each group has a ball.

3)   Players pass and move at random within their own group until the coach shouts 'change'.

4)   At this point, once the player has passed the ball, he then sprints into the parallel grid and carries on jogging.

5)   The last player with the ball dribbles at speed into the parallel grid, where the process starts again.

6)   Players do not change grids until the coach orders and then only after the ball has been passed.

19

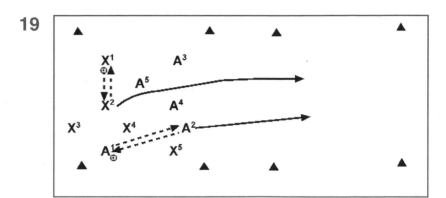

1)   Two 20 meter grids are set up, as in the above diagram.

2)   The players are divided into two equal groups and are numbered from one to five, with one group wearing a set of pinnies.

3)   The players pass and move at random until the coach shouts out 'one'. Number one is then given the ball and proceeds to play 1 - 2's with the rest of his group and in order i.e. number two followed by number three and so on.

4)   As soon as players have passed the ball back to number one, they sprint into the parallel grid and carry on jogging.

5)   When number one has played 1 - 2's with everybody, he dribbles at into the parallel grid and the process starts again.

6)   The players continue to pass at random until the coach shouts out 'two'. Number two is then given the ball and plays 1 - 2's with the rest of the group and in order i.e. number three followed by number four and so on.

7)   Once number two has played 1 - 2's with everybody, he dribbles at speed into the parallel grid and the process starts again.

8)   It is vital that players use all the space in the grid until it is their turn to play a 1 - 2.

20

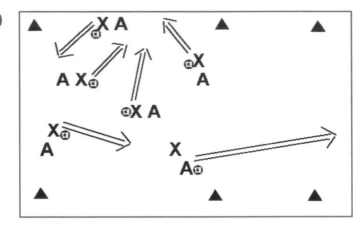

1)   Two 20 meter grids are set up, as in the above diagram.

2)   The players are divided into two equal groups, with one group wearing pinnies.

3)   All the players in one group have a ball each (in this case X's) and dribble where they like in their square.

4)   A's try to win a ball and dribble it into the other square.

5)   If an X loses his ball, he must chase back into his opponent's square to try to get the ball back.

6)   If successful, he dribbles it back into his own square.

21

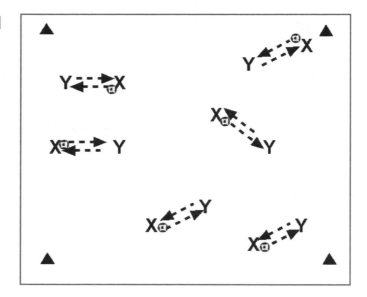

1)   A 30 meter square is set up, as in the above diagram.

2)   The players are divided into two groups, with one group
        wearing pinnies. One team (in this case X's) has a ball each.

3)   All the players jog around the area. X's run with the ball in
        their hands and play a 1 - 2 with any of the Y's. After one
        minute X's and Y's change roles.

4)   Once the system has been understood, the ball is put on the
        ground and dribbled instead. Again X's play 1 - 2's with
        Y's. After a minute the roles are reversed.

Variations
i)   X's run with the ball and throw it for Y's to head back.
ii)   X's run with the ball and throw it for Y's to volley back.
iii)   X's run with the ball and throw it for Y's to chest and volley
        back
iv)   X's run with the ball and throw it for Y's to half volley back.

22

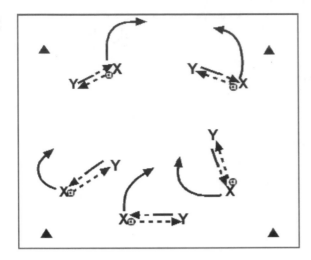

1)   A 30 meter square is set up, using four cones.

2)   The players are divided into two groups, with one group wearing pinnies. One team, in this case X's has a ball each.

3)   All the players jog around the area, filling in space. X's run with the ball in their hands, play a 1 - 2 with any of the Y's, then drop the ball for the Y to pick up.

4)   Roles are then reversed, with Y's looking for an X to play a 1 - 2 with, then dropping the ball for the X to pick up.

5)   The ball should be dropped so that players have to lean forward and pick it up after one bounce.

Variations

i)   X's dribble the ball, play a 1 - 2 with Y, then stop the ball for Y to take it on. Encourage a change of pace during this move.

ii)   X's dribble the ball. When they are about 5 meters from a Y, they call out his name, stop the ball, then sprint away.

iii) In the final variation, we ask players to multi-task. X's play a one/two with any Y. If Y passes back with his right foot, then he must turn to the left and sprint out of the space. If he plays the ball with his left foot, then he must turn to the right and sprint out of the space. After one minute, change roles.

23

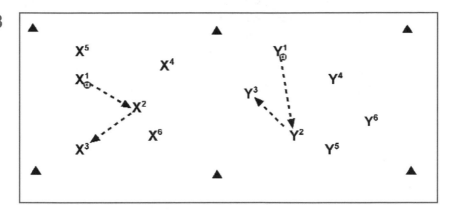

1)   Any number of players stand in two squares. One group wears a set of pinnies.

2)   Each player is given a number. Number 1 starts with the ball and passes to number 2, number 2 passes to number 3 and so on.

3)   When the ball reaches the final man, it is passed back to number 1.

4)   The ball should be passed by hand to start with but once players become familiar with the sequence, the ball should be passed by feet.

5)   When players are confident in their passing, a second ball should be introduced e.g. number 1 and number 4 start with a ball and continue to pass in sequence.

Variations
i)   Open up the centre grid line so that the groups are mixed. Continue to pass in sequence.
ii)   Once the last player is reached, pass in reverse order eg 1 2 3 4 5 6 5 4 3 2 1.

24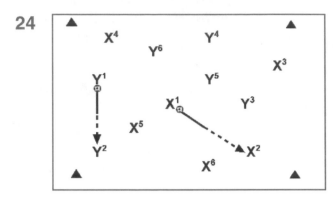

1)   A 30 meter square is marked out with four cones.

2)   Divide the players into two groups of six. One group wears a set of pinnies.

3)   Each player is given a number. Number 1 starts with the ball and passes to number 2. Number 2 passes to number 3 and so on.

4)   When the ball reaches the final man, it is passed back to number 1.

5)   After each pass, the player follows his pass, becomes a passive defender and closes down the person he has given the ball to.

6)   It is important that this is done quickly and that correct deceleration techniques are observed by the player.

7)   The attacking player drops his shoulder, dribbles round the defender, passes to the next player in the sequence and closes him down quickly.

Variations
i)   Limit the number of touches to two, then one, per player.
ii)   After passing the ball, the player closes down the person he has given the ball to, turns quickly, sprints back to his starting point, then jogs out of the space.
iii)   Five players play keep away from one defender, while passing in sequence. Play with a passive defender until a flow is established.

25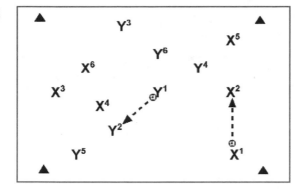

1)   A 30 meter square is marked out with four cones.

2)   Divide the players into two groups of six. One group wears a set of pinnies.

3)   Each player is given a number. Number 1 starts with the ball and passes to number 2, number 2 passes to number 3 and so on.

4)   However, number 1 does not pass to number 2 until he calls for the ball. Number 2 does not pass to number 3 until he calls for it and so on.

5)   This should encourage the player with the ball to keep his head up and observe carefully the player he is going to pass to.

Variations
i)   Complete silence. Pass in sequence but **NOBODY** is allowed to call for the ball.
ii)   Pass in sequence but after passing the ball the players form certain tasks suggested by the coach, eg they might sprint out of the space, jockey back two steps, jump to head an imaginary ball, volley right and left etc.

26

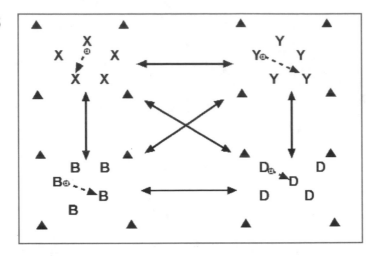

1)   Four 20 meter by 20 meter grids are set up in one half of the pitch, approximately 30 meters apart. A group of 4 to 7 players work in each grid.

2)   Each group has a ball and pass and move in their own square.

3)   On a signal from the coach, the players leave their ball and run to the facing grid. Thus groups A and B change places and grids C and D change places.

4)   This action is repeated after a pre-determined time.

5)   All the passing variations used in exercise one can be repeated in this exercise.

Variations
i)   change with the parallel group. Thus A and C change places and B and D change places.
ii)   grids change diagonally. Thus A changes with D and B changes with C.
iii)   on a signal from the coach, the ball is passed clockwise to the next group. For example group A passes to group C, group C to group D and so on. The players remain in their own square.

27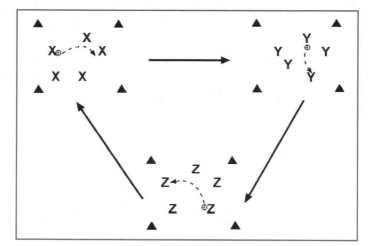

1) Three 15 meter by 15 meter grids are set up on one half of the pitch, approximately 40 meters apart. A group of 5, 6 or 7 players is in each grid.

2) X's, Y's and Z's have one ball per grid and pass and move in their own square. Start off passing by hand, then revert to feet.

3) On a signal from the coach, the players leave their ball and run to the next grid, in a clockwise direction.

4) The above action is repeated after a pre-determined time.

5) All the various ways of passing and receiving, as suggested in exercise one can be used in this warm up.

Variations
i) Players run in an counter-clockwise direction and take the ball with them.
ii) 4v1 - the last player to reach the grid becomes the defender.
iii) On a signal from the coach, the ball is passed clockwise to the next group. The players remain in their own square.

1)   A 40 meter square is used, with a 15 meter by 15 meter grid marked out at each corner, as shown in the diagram.

2)   Two groups of seven players are placed in diagonally opposite grids, with one group wearing pinnies. Each group has a ball.

3)   A ball is placed in each empty grid.

4)   Players pass and move in their own square. All the passing and receiving variations used in exercise one can be used in this exercise.

5)   On a signal from the coach, all the players move into the 40 meter square and play keep away with pinnies against plain.

6)   After three minutes, the players move back to the small grids and resume passing and moving, without opposition. Both teams move one grid, in a clockwise direction.

7)   Both teams will operate in each of the small squares in rotation, as well as play keep away in the large square.

29

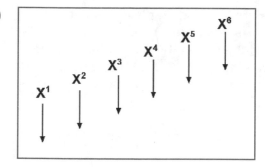

1)   Players are put into groups of six, with one ball per group

2)   The players move from one end of the pitch to the other, passing the ball by hand, rugby style. X1 runs with the ball for a short distance, then passes sideways to X2. X2 runs a short distance with the ball then passes to X3 and so on.

3)   Once the format has been understood, the ball is placed on the ground, then dribbled and passed by feet.

4)   To improve skills we can ask players to pass the ball in a specific way e.g. with the outside of the foot.

Progression One

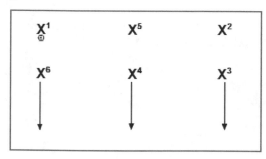

1)   The group are then put into two lines, move forward and pass the ball from the hand to anybody.

2)   Volleys from the hand and headers from the hand can be added, whilst still moving forward.

3)   Once the format has been understood and the shape kept, the ball should be placed on the ground and passed by feet.

4)   To make the exercise more difficult, players number
      themselves randomly (see diagram), but still run in the same
      shape. Whilst running they pass the ball by hand, volley pass,
      feet etc, but in sequence, ie 1 to 2, 2 to 3 and so on.

Progression

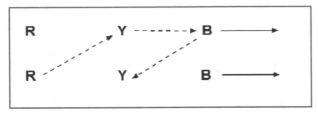

1)   The players are divided into pairs, with each pair approxi-
      mately 5 meters from those in front. Each pair is given a
      different colored pinnie.

2)   Players run forward, as in the diagram and pass the ball by
      hand, but **ONLY** to another colour. Once the format is
      established, quickly change to passing by feet.

3)   Players may change position with their partner, but not
      another color.

4)   Try to put players in the positions that they would occupy in a
      game i.e. defenders, mid-fielders and strikers.

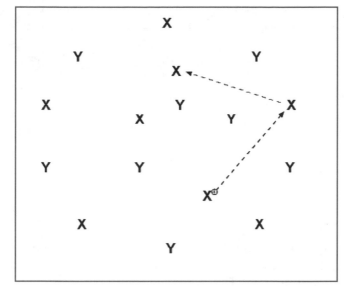

1) The players are organized into two teams of eight, with five players from each team forming a circle and the other three players from each team playing 3 v 3 inside the circle.

2) The size of the circle will depend on the age and ability of the players.

3) The 3 v 3 in the centre play keep away. They can also use
any of the perimeter players, who have to pass back to the
team that gave them the ball.

4) Encourage players to move the ball quickly and keep it simple.

5) Change the inside players every three minutes.

Variations
i) players in the centre can only use perimeter players from their own team. The perimeter player cannot pass back to the player who gave him the ball.
ii) when a centre player passes to a perimeter player from his own team, he changes places with that player. The perimeter player dribbles into the circle and has to pass to one of the centre players, before the ball can be returned to another player in the circle.

31

GAME ONE

1) The players are divided into two equal teams and play 7 v 7 on half a pitch. However, the field size can vary according to the number of players. The object of the game is to score a headed goal from a thrown pass.
2) Players pass the ball from the hands. It can only bounce once on any pass. If it bounces more than once, then it must be played with the feet like normal soccer.
3) To get the ball back into the hands to score, it has to be chipped to a teammate.
4) The ball CANNOT be picked up from the ground.
5) The player with the ball cannot be tackled and is allowed three steps when in possession.

Variations
a) Pass the ball with a kick from the hands.
b) Alternate passing from hand and feet.

GAME TWO   Diagram as for Game One

1) The aim is to score a headed goal from a thrown pass.
2) The pitch is divided into two. Each team plays normal soccer in its own half.
3) This changes to handball in the opposition half, where the ball has to be chipped to a teammate.
4) The player in possession of the ball cannot be tackled
5) The players attempt to pass accurately near the opposing goal, so that a teammate can score with a header.
6) There are no goalkeepers.

GAME THREE   Diagram as for Game One

1)   The aim is to score a point by heading the ball over an end
        line (1point) or to score a goal (2 points) by kicking the ball
        into the goal.
2)   The ball is thrown at the start.
3)   The player with the ball in his hand can only take one step.
4)   A player with the ball in his hand cannot be tackled.
5)   If the ball bounces more than once, then normal soccer is
        played.
6)   However, the player with the ball in his hand can also place it
        on the ground and play soccer.
7)   To get the ball back into the hand, it has to be chipped.

32

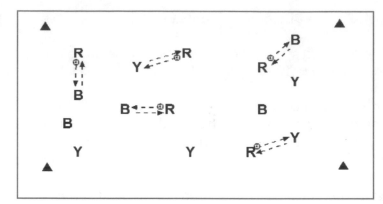

1)   A 30 meter by 20 meter grid is marked out with four cones.

2)   The players are divided into three groups, with each group in different colored pinnies.

3)   Players in one group have a ball each and dribble where they like, playing 1 - 2's with the other two groups.

4)   After two minutes, another color takes the balls and the same action is repeated.

Variations
i)   reds throw the balls for yellows and blues to head back.
ii)   reds throw the balls for yellows and blues to volley back.
iii)   red plays the ball to a yellow. He passes to a blue, who returns the ball to the original red.
iv)   as above but red throws the ball for yellow to control on his chest and volley to blue. Blue returns the ball to the original red.
v)   red passes to yellow, yellow passes to blue, blue passes back first time to yellow and yellow returns the ball to red. To achieve this sequence there must be lots of talking.

33

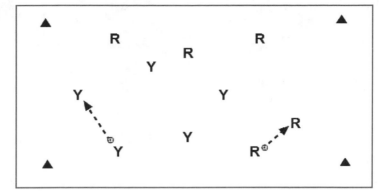

1)   A 30 meter by 20 meter grid is marked out with four cones.

2)   The players are divided into two groups, each group having a ball and in different colored pinnies.

3)   Players start off passing by hand and to their own color i.e. red to red, yellow to yellow.

4)   After a few minutes, change to passing by feet.

5)   Once a flow has been established, change to passing in sequence i.e. yellow to red, red to yellow.

Variation

i)   as for 5), but yellows have two touches and reds have three touches. Quickly reduce this to one touch and two touches.

ii)   Red passes to a yellow, follows his pass and closes the yellow down. Yellow has to immediately find another red with a one touch pass. This red then dribbles the ball, finds another yellow and the process starts again.

iii) Red passes to yellow and closes the yellow down. Yellow has to find another yellow with a one touch pass. Yellow 2 now dribbles the ball, passes to a red and closes him down. The red now has to find another red with a one touch pass and the process starts again.

34

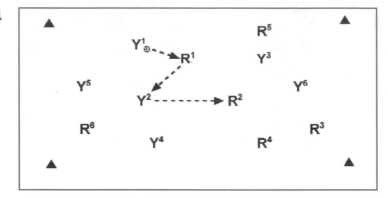

1)   Set up two 30 meter by 15 meter grids side by side. This
     practice will require a minimum of 12 players and a maximum
     of 16.

2)   The players are divided into two groups, with each group in
     different colored pinnies.

3)   The two groups pass and move using three balls.

4)   When a flow has been established, give each player a
     number. Number one yellow passes to number one red,
     number two red passes to number two yellow and so on.
     Start off with one ball and throw by hand, and when the
     sequence has been established, use the feet and use two
     more balls.

Variation
Yellows pass in sequence i.e. 1 to 2, 2 to 3 and so on, whilst reds
become passive defenders and close down their opposite number.
Thus red one will close down yellow one when he receives the ball,
red two will close down yellow two when he receives the ball and so
on. Encourage yellows to open out and take the ball on their back
foot or receive the ball with the inside or outside of the front foot and
take it off line.

Progression

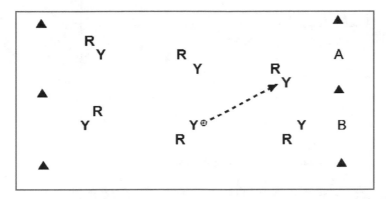

1)   Reds in grid A play with reds in grid B, whilst yellows in grid A
      work with yellows in grid B.

2)   Both teams try to work the ball from one grid to the other,
      without the ball being intercepted. All players have to work in
      their assigned zones.

3)   If one group manages three consecutive passes in their zone
      and this is then repeated by the same colour in the other
      zone, then that team wins a point.

35

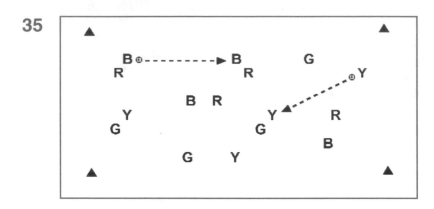

1) A 40 meter by 30 meter grid is marked out with four cones, as in the diagram.

2) The players are divided into four groups, with each group wearing a different set of pinnies.

3) The teams start by playing handball, with reds versus blues and yellows versus greens.

4) Once a flow has been established, change to passing by feet.

5) To make players think, the coach should keep changing the pairings i.e. reds versus yellows and greens versus blues.

Progression

a) Some direction is then put on the practice, with reds versus blues playing vertically and yellows versus greens playing horizontally. To score players have to dribble over the end line they are attacking and place a foot on top of the ball. Once again, the coach should keep changing the pairings.

b) The colors should then be joined, with reds playing with blues and yellows playing with greens. Start with keep ball and progress with end ball. However the ball must be passed in sequence - thus red will play to blue, blue to red and yellow to green, green to yellow.

36

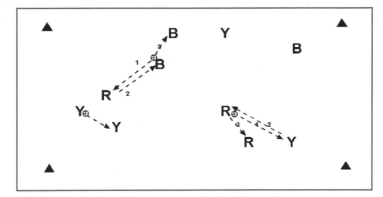

1)   A 40 meter by 30 meter grid is marked out with four cones.

2)   The players are divided into three groups, with each group having a ball and in different colored pinnies.

3)   Groups start off passing by hand and to their own color, but quickly change to passing by feet.

4)   Once a flow has been established, players may also pass to a player of another color, who must return the ball first time to the player who gave him the ball.

Variations

i)   players play a 1 - 2 with a different color, then pass to one of his team-mates e.g. blue passes to red, red plays back to blue first time and blue passes to another red.

ii)   players pass in sequence i.e. red to yellow, yellow to blue, blue to red. To make players think, the coach should keep changing the sequence.

iii)   two colors combine to play keep away from the other color, making it 10 v 5. If the defenders win the ball, they give it back to the attackers. Play for three minutes then change the defending team.

37

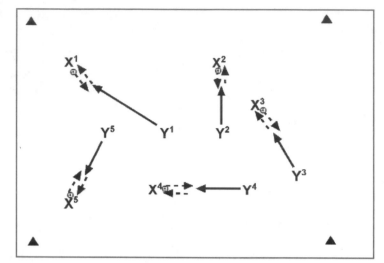

1)   A 30 meter by 30 meter grid is marked out with four cones. Any number of players can work in the grid.

2)   Players are divided into pairs, with one ball for each pair. In the diagram, Y's are the working players and X's have the ball.

3)   Y's position themselves between 10 and 12 meters from their partners. When ready, they sprint to their partners, play a 1 - 2, **THEN STAY WHERE THEY ARE**.

4)   X's then dribble to another area of the grid. When they have fully recovered, Y's sprint again to play a 1 - 2 with their partner.

5)   Y's must concentrate on the correct technique for acceleration. However, with so many pairs, it is unlikely that they will be able to sprint in a straight line.

6)   Work for one minute, then change roles.

Variations
The sprinting player starts:
i)   standing with feet parallel
ii)   standing with left foot forward

iii)   standing with right foot forward
iv)   on one knee
v)   lying face down
vi)   lying face down, then roll over and get up
vii)   lying on back
viii)   sitting
ix)   on hands and knees
x)   in a four point position, two hands and two feet on the ground
xi)   in a three point position, two feet and one hand
xii)   squatting

The serving player throws the ball for player to:

- head
- volley
- chest and volley
- half volley
- thigh and volley

38

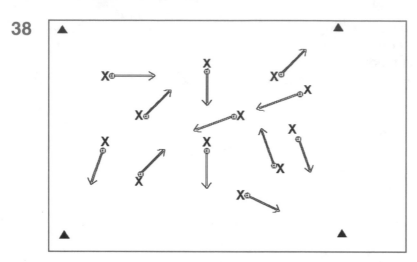

1)   A 30 meter by 30 meter grid is set up with four cones.

2)   The players have a ball each and dribble inside the grid.

3)   The coach should encourage dribbling into space, different fakes and moves and a change in rhythm.

4)   Once a flow has been established, the practice develops in the following way. When players pass to each other, they:

a)   exchange balls
b)   stop their ball and take the other one
c)   stop their ball, jump in the air and take the other one
d)   stop their ball, touch the ground with both hands, then take the other one
e)   stop the ball, roll it back with the sole of the foot, then take the other one
f)   stop the ball, sit down, get up quickly and take the other one
g)   dribble round each other, stop the ball and take the other one
h)   stop the ball and take the other one away at pace
i)   stop the ball, jump and shoulder charge the opponent, then take his ball
j)   stop the ball, jockey back three steps, then take the other one
k)   stop the ball, run to touch the other ball, then run back to their own

Once again, the list is endless and is up to the coach's imagination.

39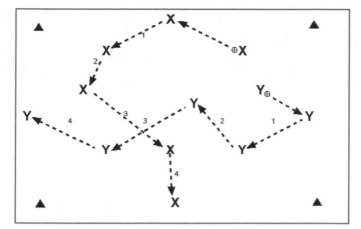

1)   A 40 meter square is marked out with four cones.

2)   The players are divided into two groups, each group having a ball and in different colored pinnies.

3)   Two players from each group stand on opposite sides of the square.

4)   One team plays across the field, the other plays up and down.

5)   Each group has a minimum of three passes to get from one side of the grid to the other.

6)   The final pass is played to the end player, who plays it back first time to any of his players, apart from the one who gave him the ball.

7)   Then with a minimum of three passes, the ball has to be passed to the opposite end player.

Variations
i)   the person who passes to the end player changes places with him.
ii)   the two teams play keep away against each other inside the grid. The aim is to pass the ball from one end player to the other, without the opposition intercepting. If they do, then they attempt to do the same with their end players.

40

1)   A grid 50 meters by 25 meters is marked out with four cones.

2)   The players are divided into two equal teams, with one team in pinnies.

3)   Two players from each team stand on opposite sides of the rectangle.

4)   One team plays across the field, whilst the other plays up and down.

5)   The teams play keep away against each other. The aim is to pass the ball to an end player, then transfer it to the other end player.

6)   By experimenting with the shape of the pitch, different problems will be posed, since X's will be playing on a long, narrow pitch and Y's on a short, wide pitch.

7)   The side players may move up and down their lines to receive the ball.

8)   Work for five minutes, then switch directions.

Variations

i)   The side players have to pass back in, one touch.

ii)   The person who passes to the side player changes places with him.

iii)   Side players cannot pass back to the player who passed to them.

41

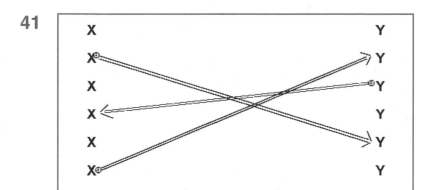

1)   Players line up as in the diagram, about 20 meters apart - three balls for twelve players. With more players, the number of balls should be increased.

2)   Those with the balls dribble across to players on the opposite side and take their place.

3)   It is important that players change tempo whilst dribbling.

4)   Players must be aware of others, as well as their own ball.

Variations
i)   Players dribble half-way across, call the name of a free player and pass to him.
ii)   Players dribble, then pass with the outside of the foot.
iii)   Players dribble, perform a trick half way across then pass to a free player.
iv)   Players dribble across, go round a free player, then play a little pass into his running path.
v)   Players dribble half-way across, call the name of a free player, play a 1 - 2 with him, and then pass the ball into his running path.
vi)   Players dribble half way across, call the name of a free player, and then pass to him. Before receiving the pass, this player has to perform a pre-determined skill. This could be a jump to head an imaginary ball, touch the ground with both hands, volley right or left, move away and come back to the ball etc.

42

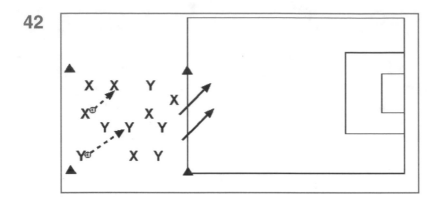

1)   A 30 meter square is marked out with four cones, on one side of the half-way line. A larger area, such as half a pitch, is marked out next to it.

2)   The players are divided into two groups, with each group having a ball and in different colored pinnies.

3)   Players start off in the small area, moving and passing to their own color.

4)   At the coach's signal, the players move into the large area and carry on passing, but with all the passes over 10 meters.

5)   At the coach's signal, the players return to the small area and carry on passing as before.

6)   All the passing and receiving variations used in exercise one can be used in this part of the warm up.

Progression

a)   The two teams play keep away against each other in the small area. A supply of balls should be made available at the side of the pitch.

b)   On a signal from the coach the teams move into the large area and carry on competing. The team in possession when the coach shouts 'change' has responsibility for bringing the ball into the large area. The opposition cannot challenge whilst this is happening.

c)   After a few minutes, when the coach gives the signal, play is brought back to the small area by the team in possession and the competition continues.

d)   Two small goals are placed at either end of the pitch in the large area. The teams play keep away in the small area, but attack one goal and defend the other on the large pitch.

43

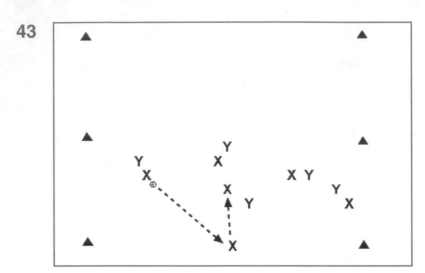

1)   Set up two 40 meter by 20 meter grids, side by side.

2)   The players are divided into two groups, with each group in different colored pinnies.

3)   Each team has one player on an end line and at opposite sides of the playing area.

4)   X's try to maintain possession in their half of the field and can make use of their end player. However, he must pass the ball, one touch, back to a player in his team.

5)   If Y's gain possession they pass to their end player and the teams switch to the other half of the playing area, where the process starts again.

Variations

i)   The teams defend the end line where their player is situated and try to prevent the other team from dribbling the ball over that line. The end player acts as the last line of defense. Teams can still pass to their players on the end line and he **CANNOT** be challenged if in possession of the ball.

ii)   The teams attack the end line where their player is situated and attempt to dribble over that line. The end players are used for support and set up play.

44

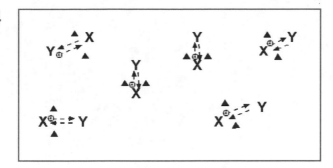

1)   Several small arches are placed randomly on quarter of a
      pitch.

2)   The players are divided into pairs (X and Y). X has a ball.

3)   Y runs to any arch and X follows. He plays a 1 - 2 with Y
      through the arch.

4)   Y then runs to another arch and X follows. Once again, a
      1 - 2 is played through the arch and the process starts
      again.

5)   Roles are reversed after two minutes.

Variations

i)   The first pass is played through the arch, whilst the return
      pass is made outside the arch.

ii)   The ball is passed three times through the arch, so that each
      time the start of the move alternates between X and Y.

iii) One player is designated the attacker and the other the
      defender. The attacker tries to dribble through as many
      arches as possible in one minute. He cannot score through
      the same arch twice in a row.

45

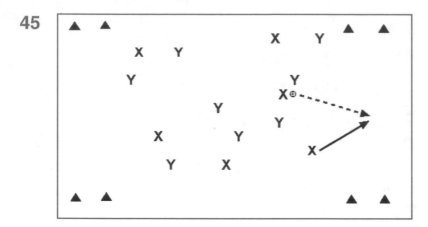

1)   A 30 meter by 20 meter grid is set up, with two five meter zones marked out at either end.

2)   The players are divided into two teams, with one team in pinnies.

3)   The teams play a simplified form of rugby and can only throw and catch the ball. Running with the ball is not allowed and there is no tackling. Defenders can only win the ball by interceptions.

4)   The offensive team attempt to place the ball down in their attacking zone. Players **CANNOT** stand and wait in the end zone, but have to move into it as the ball is passed.

Variations
i)   Players pass by hand but the last pass into the zone has to be a header.
ii)   Players volley pass from the hand instead of throw.
iii)   A player from each team is placed in one of the outer zones and is free to move anywhere in it. The players from his team attempt to pass the ball to him. If successful, the zone player transfers the ball to the opposing team. Start off passing by hand, and then change to passing by feet.

46

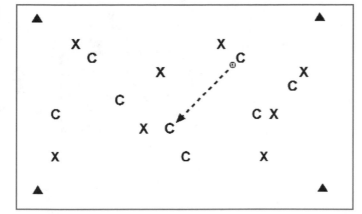

1)   A 30 meter by 20 meter grid is marked out with four cones.

2)   The players are divided into two groups, with one group in pinnies.

3)   In the above diagram, C's are the catchers and X's the free runners.

4)   C's have a ball between them and can either dribble it one-handed or pass it.

5)   When they get near an X, they can throw the ball up and head it, with the aim of hitting one of the X's.

6)   The C's see how many X's they can hit with headers in three minutes, then change roles.

Variations
i)   Use more than one ball.
ii)   Half volley the ball to hit opponents.

47

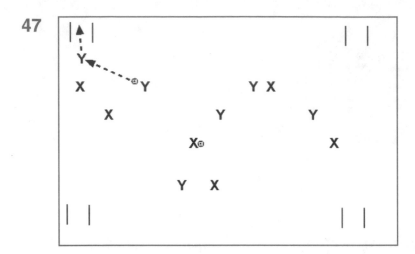

1)   A 30 meter by 20 meter grid is marked out with a goal at each corner, consisting of two poles about one meter apart.

2)   The players are divided into two groups, with one group in pinnies.

3)   Each team has two goals to attack and two goals to defend.

4)   The ball is passed by hand. Running with the ball is not allowed and there is no tackling.

5)   A goal is scored if a player scores direct with a header, or throws the ball up himself to head a goal.

Variations
i)   Man to man marking
ii)   Teams attack two diagonal goals and defend two diagonal goals.

48

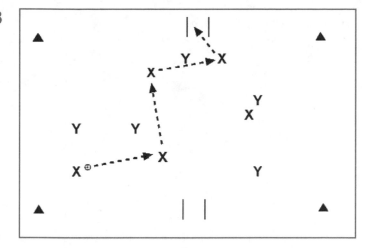

1)   A 40 meter square is marked out with goals at each end.

2)   The players are divided into two equal teams, with one team in pinnies.

3)   The game is played like handball and players throw and catch using their hands. Goals can only be scored from headers.

4)   However, a player can only score from a thrown pass. He cannot throw the ball up and head it himself.

5)   There are no goalkeepers.

6)   Once a player catches the ball, he is limited to three steps and then must pass.

49

1)   A 30 meter square is marked out with four cones.

2)   The players are divided into two teams, with one team in pinnies. Each team has a ball.

3)   The teams compete to see which one can make the greatest number of passes in a specified time.

4)   Each pass must be over five meters.

5)   Players of one team must not interfere with the passing of the other team.

6)   Players must not pass back to the player who gave them the ball.

7)   Players must keep moving all the time.

8)   Two referees will be needed to adjudicate.

50

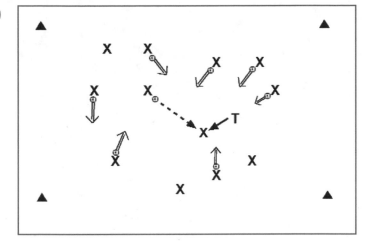

1) A 20 meter square is marked out with four cones.

2) Eight players in the square have a ball each and four players do not.

3) A tagger, without a ball, tries to tag one of the four players who do not have a ball.

4) Players with a ball cannot be tagged.

5) Therefore, the aim is for the twelve players to pass amongst themselves, in order to avoid getting tagged.

6) If a player gets tagged, he becomes the new tagger.

7) For larger groups use more balls and two taggers.

8) Start off passing by hand and when a flow has been established, change to passing by feet.

51

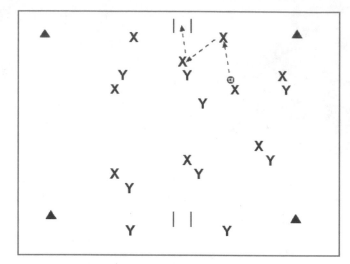

1) A 30 meter square is marked out with goals at each end.

2) The players are divided into two equal teams, with one team in pinnies.

3) Two players from each team are positioned on a goal line, as in the diagram. These players may move along the goal line, but may not enter the square.

4) The game is played like handball and players throw and catch using their hands.

5) To score a goal the ball must first be passed to an end player. He returns the ball for one of his team to head or volley at goal.

6) If this sequence breaks down, the ball has to be passed to an end player, before another header or volley can be attempted.

7) Change the end player every time a goal is scored.

52

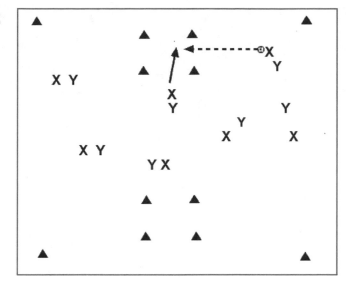

1) A 40 meter square is marked out with four cones. Two 5 meter squares are marked out inside the large square. For greater numbers, the outer square can be enlarged.

2) The players are divided into two teams, with one team in pinnies. Each team has one small square to attack and one to defend.

3) The players start passing by hand. However, they are not allowed to dribble the ball or take more than two steps when in possession.

4) One of the players of the team in possession must run into his team's square at the right moment to receive a pass.

5) The ball must not be bounced to the player in the square, and if it is dropped, then the goal does not count.

6) Defenders are not allowed in their defensive square

7) Once a flow has been established, change to passing by feet.

53

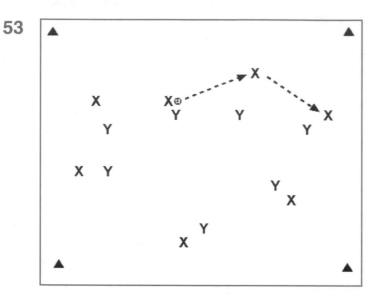

1) A 40 meter square is marked out with four cones.

2) The players are divided into two teams, with one team in pinnies.

3) The teams play keep away and attempt to achieve **SEVEN** consecutive passes.

4) However, they only score a point if the seventh pass is chipped to a team member and is caught. If the ball is dropped, then the score is not counted.

5) Play two touch so that ball circulation is quick.

Variation
Put a goalkeeper on each side and the seventh pass has to be played to him. Any type of pass will do, as long as it reaches him and he collects it cleanly.

54

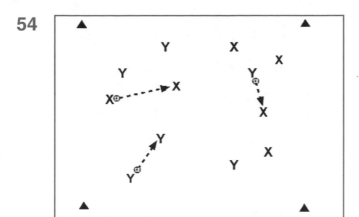

1)   A 30 meter square is marked out with four cones.

2)   The players are divided into two groups, with one group in pinnies.

3)   Each group has a ball. In addition there is a third ball, which is either another color, a different size or has distinctive markings.

4)   X's pass their ball randomly amongst themselves whilst Y's do the same thing.

5)   The additional ball, however, is passed alternately between the groups. Thus the yellow ball will be passed from X to Y, Y to X and so on.

6)   Encourage players to call clearly and move about the grid with their heads up.

Variations

i)   Players have three touches with their own ball but only two touches with the alternate ball. This could be reduced to two touches and one touch, depending on the ability of the group.

ii)   If the group is larger than 12 then divide the players into three groups, with each in different colored pinnies. All three groups have a ball each, which they pass randomly amongst themselves. The alternate ball, however, has to be passed in sequence i.e. green to blue, blue to yellow, and yellow to green.

55

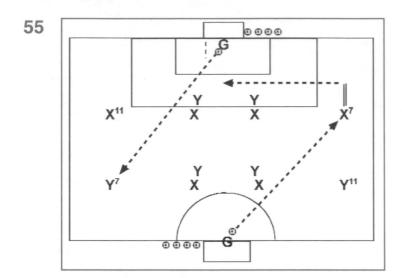

1)   12 players and 2 goalkeepers line up on half a pitch, as in the diagram. Both goalkeepers have a large supply of balls.

2)   Two defenders mark the two strikers from both teams.

3)   The four wide players, however, are unmarked.

4)   X's goalkeeper starts the action by throwing the ball to X7. He controls the ball, dribbles at pace to the goal line and crosses for his two attackers to attempt to score.

5)   When this phase of play ends, Y's goalkeeper repeats the action by throwing the ball to Y7. Y7 dribbles to the goal line and crosses for his two attackers to attempt to score.

6)   Again when this phase of play ends, X's goalkeeper throws to X11 and the action is repeated on the left-hand side.

7)   Work for five minutes then change the wide players.

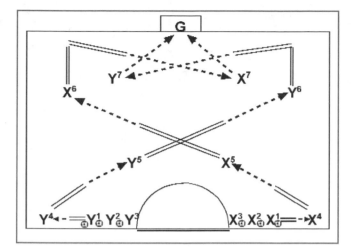

1) A minimum of 14 players is required for this exercise.

2) The starting players line up on the half way line, with a ball each.

3) X1 passes to X4, follows his pass and takes X4's place.

4) X4 passes to X5 and follows his pass.

5) X5 passes to X6 and follows his pass.

6) X6 dribbles to the goal line and crosses for X7 to attempt a strike at goal.

7) X6 takes X7's place and so becomes the next striker.

8) X7 collects his ball after the strike and joins the queue on the half way line.

9) As soon as the ball reaches X5, Y1 starts, passes to Y4 etc, on the other side of the pitch.

Variations
i) Add a defender.
ii) Keep the same strikers.

57

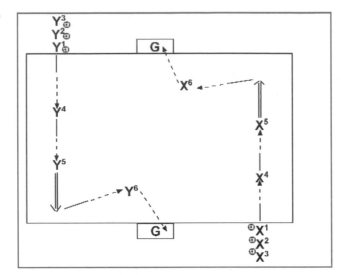

1)   A minimum of 12 players and 2 goalkeepers line up on half a pitch, as in the diagram.

2)   X's on the half way line and Y's on the goal line have a ball each.

3)   X1 and Y1 start at the same time. X1 passes to X4 and follows his pass whilst Y1 passes to Y4 and follows his pass.

4)   X4 takes the ball on the back foot, passes to X5 and follows his pass.

5)   X5 crosses for X6 to have a strike at goal. X5 then takes X6's place.

6)   X6 collects his ball and joins the back of Y's line.

7)   Y's carry out the same procedure down their side of the field and Y6 joins the back of X's line, after his attempted strike at goal.

8)   It is important to keep a fast momentum going. Therefore, as soon as X4 and Y4 have passed to X5 and Y5 respectively and X1 and Y1 have taken their places, the next balls are passed in by X2 and Y2.

Variations

i)   Add a defender to mark the striking player.

ii)   Work the other way down the pitch so that the ball is crossed
        from the left instead of the right. X's will therefore start on the
        goal line and Y's on the half way line.

58

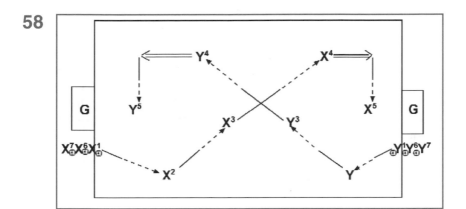

1)   Players work across half a pitch. If there are more than 16
        players, the number of stations can be increased or the
        practice can be changed to a full pitch.

2)   X's and Y's start at the same time. X1 passes to X2, follows
        his pass and takes X2's. Y1 passes to Y2, follows his pass
        and takes Y2's place.

3)   X2 passes to X3 and follows his pass. X3 passes to X4 and
        follows his pass.

4)   X4 dribbles and crosses for X5 to attempt a strike at goal. X4
        takes X5's place and becomes the next striker.

5)   X5, in the meantime, collects his ball and joins group Y.

6)   Y's work down their side of the pitch and Y5 joins the back of
        X's group after his strike at goal.

7)   It is important to keep a fast momentum going. As soon as X1
        and Y1 take X2 and Y2's place, X6 and Y6 pass in the next
        balls.

59

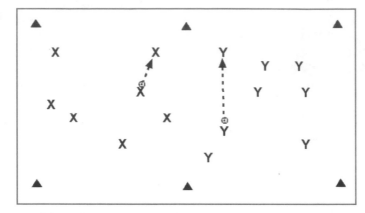

It is possible, with a little imagination, to combine all three elements of the warm up - dynamic flexibility, running technique and specific soccer movement - in one practice.

1)   Two 20 meter squares are set up side by side, as in the above diagram.

2)   The players are divided into two teams, with one team in pinnies. Each team has a ball and operates in a separate grid.

3)   Players pass and move in their area. On a signal from the coach, the players stop and the player in possession of the ball has to demonstrate a dynamic flexibility exercise, which the rest of the group copies.

4)   When the coach is satisfied that the exercise has been carried out correctly, players continue to pass and move.

5)   This process continues until all the major areas of the body have been warmed and stretched.

Progression One

a)   The coach then introduces various acceleration exercises without the ball. When he is satisfied the movements are being carried out correctly, the ball is reintroduced. Players now pass but, after passing the ball, have to accelerate into space.

b)   Deceleration exercises are then revised without the ball.
      When the coach is satisfied with technique, the ball is then
      reintroduced. Players pass and move, but this time act as
      passive defenders and quickly close down the player they
      have passed to.

c)   Finally, lateral movements are practiced without the ball.
      Again, when satisfied the players are performing the move-
      ments correctly, the coach reintroduces the ball. After passing
      the ball, the players shuffle sideways three steps, backwards
      three steps, jockey three steps etc, before accelerating into
      space.

Progression Two

In the final part of the warm up, the central cones are removed and a
grid 40 meters by 20 meters is established. The two teams play keep
ball and the usual restrictions of three touch, two touch etc are used
to speed up the action.

60

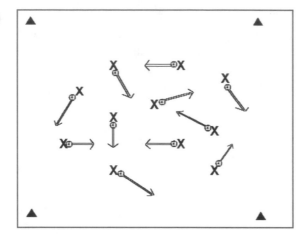

The final practice is for those who have to train with poor ground
conditions, or limited space, such as the side of the pitch.
Demanding technical exercises are not possible, but by being
creative, an effective warm up involving a ball, can be used prior to
the training session.

1)   A 30 meter square is marked out with four cones. Each play
        er has a ball and moves freely in the square. Whilst running,
        the players perform the following exercises with the ball:

a)   Pass the ball from left hand to right hand around the body
        and vice versa.
b)   Throw the ball up, jump and catch it.
c)   Throw the ball from one hand to the other.
d)   Throw the ball up, clap hands, jump and catch it.
e)   Keep the ball in the hand and kick it with the instep, toe, thigh
        etc
f)   Throw the ball up, bounce it off the chest and catch it.
g)   Throw the ball up, bounce it off the head and catch it.
h)   Throw the ball up, bounce it off the thigh and catch it.
i)   Throw the ball up, bounce it off the right thigh, left thigh and
        catch it.
j)   Throw the ball up, kick it with the instep and catch it.
k)   Throw the ball up, bounce it off the outside of the ankle and
        catch it.
l)   Throw the ball up, bounce it off the chest, knock it up with the
        thigh and catch it.
m)   Throw the ball up, knock it up with the shoulder and catch it.

Conclusion

This, then, is how I believe players should warm up for soccer. As the game progresses, players are given less time and space on the ball, so it is vital that we develop soccer players who can control the ball quickly, accelerate, decelerate and move laterally and are able to make correct and rapid decisions. I feel the time to reinforce these basic requirements is during the warm up.

Why then should rapid decision-making be part of the warm up? I feel we need to know the motor learning processes involved in soccer, which are very different from closed skill sports such as golf, gymnastics and archery. Soccer is an open skilled game which takes place in an unpredictable environment where situations are continually changing. How players cope with these changes depends on how they receive, process and then react to the information provided. Too often, we teach players the skills of the game in predictable situations e.g. dribbling around cones which do not move, instead of in a square, where other players are moving and so have to be avoided. I believe it is necessary, even in the warm up, to put players in decision-making situations, so that the thought processes are speeded up and players are encouraged to select the correct responses, which will be essential once the game starts.

During a match, players receive vast amounts of information at the same time and this has to be processed, put in sequence and then the correct motor program selected. I do not feel the vast majority of warm ups that I observe, even at the highest level, stimulate the brain and nervous system and prepare for the match ahead. Too often, after getting warm, body temperature is allowed to drop through static stretching and then much of the ball work is either performed stationary or in a moving situation which does not require anticipation, decision-making or an awareness of space. As a result, reaction time, which is the interval between an unanticipated stimulus and the beginning of the response, is not practiced and so decision-making at the start of the game can be slow and often incorrect.

It is also vital that the coach picks up incorrect technique and movement during the warm up, whether it is the dynamic flexibility, running drills or ball work. It has been stated that "it takes 350 repetitions to learn a motor program and 3500 repetitions to correct a bad motor program". It therefore makes sense to ensure that players are performing the correct techniques whilst warming up. The coach does not have to be an athletics guru to observe correct running movements. He just needs to make sure that basic movements are followed, particularly with regard to acceleration and the five-step pattern and that any mistakes are corrected immediately.

A further reminder to coaches is that the warm up before a game should continue until shortly before the start of the match. When exercise stops, the temperature of the previously activated muscles decreases quickly and is back to pre-exercise level after about 15 minutes, at which point the benefits from the warm up are lost. A considerable loss of temperature is also likely to occur at half time. It is therefore advisable for players to perform some light activities immediately before kick off and immediately before the start of the second half. Exercises such as patters on the spot or go for your gun would be ideal. Even a coordination ladder, appropriately placed in the tunnel, could be an innovative way to concentrate the mind and prepare the players for what is to come.

Another area of concern is the warm up performed by the substitutes. From my experience it usually consists of a jog to the corner flag and a series of static stretches that are performed whilst watching the game. This is totally inadequate and certainly does not prepare the player for the rigors of a game if called off the bench. I would expect the substitutes to perform dynamic flexibility exercises, running exercises and exercises with the ball, all at a high tempo. This would ensure that if a player were brought on, he would be able to adapt to the pace of the game straightaway.

I hope by reading this book you have learned something about warm ups and have lots of new ideas on how to begin your training sessions. However, I have to emphasize that this book is only a starting point. Like other aspects of life, the game of soccer is evolving rapidly all the time and what is valid today could be out of date tomorrow. The coach must therefore adapt to soccer's ever-changing demands, in order to stay competitive. It is also vital that we produce coaches who are creative, innovative, forward thinking and flexible and who don't blindly repeat what they did as players.

From a personal point of view, I strongly believe in the Spanish method of integral training, which, as far as possible, combines the technical, tactical and physical. I feel that the warm up should not be excluded from this approach and that once the body is warm, players should be put into a soccer environment where they have to be aware of time, space and opposition. There is no doubt the coach has to be creative when thinking up new warm up practices, but if he wants to keep the attention of the players, then he must work with a ball and create new problems for them to solve. This not only motivates, but produces a coaching style which educates at the same time!

Bibliography

1) Dr Raymond Verheijen, **Conditioning for Soccer**. Reedswain 1998

2) Peter Schreiner, **Coordination, Agility and Speed Training for Soccer**. Reedswain 2000

3) Bangsbo, **Fitness Training for Football - A Scientific Approach**. HO+Storm, Bagsvaerd 1994.

4) Karl-Heinz Heddergott, **New Football Manual**. Limpert 1976

5) Thomas Kurtz, **Stretching Scientifically**. Stadion Publishing Company 1991

6) Pavel Tsatsouline, **Beyond Stretching**, Dragoon Door Publication

7) Angela Calder, **Australian Institute of Sports Flexibility parts 1,2 and 3, Strength and Conditioning** Sports Coach Summer, Autumn and Winter 2000.

8) Rutledge and Faccioni, **Dynamic Warm Ups**. Sports Coach - volume 24 no1 2001.

9) Dean Benton, **Sprint Running Needs Of Field Sports Athletes: A New Perspective**. Sports Coach - volume 24 no2 2001.

10) **The Role of Dynamic Flexibility in Warm Up**. SAQ European Symposium June 10 and 11 2000.

11) Peter Schokman, **A review of warm up for field team sports: putting the theory into practice**. Sports Coach Autumn 1999.

12) Steve Myrland, **Straight Ahead Speed**. Performance Conditioning for Soccer. Vol 2 Number 9 1996.

13) Neil Sedgwick, **Stride Length and Frequency**. Performance Conditioning for Soccer Volume 4 no 3

14) Steve Myrland, **Soccer Acceleration: Gaining First Gear**. The Complete Guide to Soccer Conditioning.

15) Larry Gardner, **Designing a Summer Soccer Conditioning Camp**. Performance Conditioning for Soccer Volume 7 no1

Equipment Used in this Book
Available from Reedswain

Accu-Arches

Agility Poles

Tall Cones

Coordination Ladder

Disc Cones

Also Available from Reedswain

Also Available from Reedswain

#185 **Conditioning for Soccer** ————————
by Raymond Verheijen
$19.95

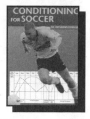

#188 **300 Innovative Soccer Drills** ————————
by Roger Wilkinson and Mick Critchell
$14.95

#290 **Practice Plans for Effective
         Training** ————————————————
by Ken Sherry
$14.95

#787 **Attacking Schemes and
         Training Exercises** ————————————
by Eugenio Fascetti and Romedio Scaia
$14.95

#788 **Zone Play** ————————————————
by Angelo Pereni and Michele di Cesare
$14.95

#792 **120 Competitive Games and
         Exercises** ————————————————
by Nicola Pica
$14.95

#793 **Coaching the 5-3-2** ————————
by Eugenio Fascetti and Romedio Scaia
$14.95

www.reedswain.com or 800-331-5191